# The Last Struggle With The Mafia

## by

## Cesare Mori

The Last Struggle With The Mafia

by

Cesare Mori

Introduction

by

Kerry Bolton

ISBN-13: 978-1-910881-38-5


Black House Publishing Ltd
Kemp House
152 City Road
London
United Kingdom
EC1V 2NX
www.blackhousepublishing.com

Email: info@blackhousepublishing.com

# Translator's Note

In the English version certain omissions have been made and in some places the order has been changed. One of the objects of the Italian original is to defend Signor Mori's admittedly somewhat drastic administration against criticism by his own countrymen, but this controversy does not concern English readers and the text seems more effective without it. I have also ventured to compress some of the passages dealing with general subjects, and I have reduced the quotations from other writers and from the author's own speeches and from historical works. The direct narrative of Signor Mori's thrilling achievement has been kept intact.

Orlo Williams

March 1933

# Contents

# Introduction

This thrilling narrative about the destruction of the Mafia by the first and only man who has ever achieved that takes the reader back to a time when these infamous brigands ruled Sicily since the medieval era, and succeeded in overcoming all efforts to establish peace and prosperity on the island. The Mafia of legend is well-known, but mostly in its American form. Far less is known about the Mafia at the place from which it arose: Sicily. Right up to the mid-1920s Sicily, if comparisons are to be made with the American situation, was more like the Wild West than 'Roaring Twenties' Chicago. This is not the Mafia of the 'The Sopranos' image, nor were bootlegging and prostitution the enterprises of the American Mafiosi Sicilian cousins. The Sicilian Mafia thrived in rural villages, while Capone and Luciano et al built their criminal empires in the American cities. Bootlegging was the primary activity in Prohibition era America, while in Sicily goat, cattle and sheep rustling and grain theft were the mainstay of the brigands. This was no triviality in Sicily. The extent of the Mafia's activities was such that large landowners and peasants alike lived in fear, and paid their tribute to the Mafia, and the economy and agricultural production of Sicily was seriously compromised. There was nothing of a Robin Hood nature about the Mafia; no romantic aura for the Sicilian village and country folk, despite continuing efforts to portray it as such.

As in the USA however, the Sicilian Mafia extracted protection money, as tolls and taxes, corrupted local politicians, kidnapped, blackmailed, indulged in clan feuds, and had major shootouts with police. Livestock were taken from peasants and large landowners alike, on multiple occasions, as ransom. Unlike the USA, the brigands had many escape routes in the villages and countryside, they could impose themselves on any household when hiding from police, and could disappear into the mountains and hills. Some of these bandit gangs held out for more than a decade in the hill-country, eluding the police and terrorising local villagers, estate owners and peasants at will.

Cesare Mori changed within a few years what has become a tradition in Sicily for centuries. Had Mori been an American instead of an Italian whose career culminated during the Fascist era, he would today be lauded alongside Elliott Ness as one of the greatest crime fighters in history. Hence, this edition of his memoirs is a valuable contribution to understanding the era.

Mori was unlike any other policeman. While the focus, when mentioned at all, has been on clichéd allegations of Mori's 'brutal' war against banditry, this book places the matter into context, something that is seldom done by the critics. Even in Mori's time, and in Fascist Italy, he was criticised for the harshness of his methods; which is to say, his effectiveness. He also had a political enemy in Alfredo Cucco, the head of the Black Shirts in Palermo, who was the source of some of the allegations against Mori's methods, and went as far as having his men demonstrate against Mori. Cucco was expelled from the party for corruption and his branch dissolved. The Mafia also had its partisans spreading smears against Mori. However, what these memoirs make clear is that Mori was engaged in a guerrilla war, quite unlike the situation of the FBI in dealing with the Mafia in the USA. The brigands knew the villages and the land. They eluded the police and hid out in the hills and mountains of Sicily for years. They were well–armed bands, able to ambush police pursuers, and skilled in guerrilla tactics.

Mori acted on multiple levels, not only with gunfire and roundups. He formed the first trans-provisional police in Sicily. He enacted laws that enabled suspects to be rounded up and tried *en masse*, and with evidence painstakingly collected and swiftly assessed. The 'associations' of Mafiosi were destroyed by criminalising associating with bandits. Other than this however, Mori did much more. He collected information on the character of the Mafia, going *incognito* among the villagers and peasants, until he became a legend, feared almost as a phantom by the brigands who did not know where Mori might be lurking. Mori most of all gave Sicilians, landowners, villagers, peasants, the courage to stand up to the Mafia; to the extent that individuals were empowered to shoot Mafiosi who threatened them, their families or property. Such action was even rewarded with medals of civic service. The mass of people, terrorised for centuries, and afraid to speak, were empowered. Auxiliaries of citizens were formed. Families affected by the arrest of kin for banditry were provided assistance where needed by the Syndicate of Agriculture Workers and other state agencies. Mori instituted programmes for cattle breeding, which had been ruined by years of Mafia theft and extortion. He established a commission drawn from all sections of the community to study the Mafia. Not only was he called the 'Iron Prefect', but among the masses of grateful people, they spoke of the 'Peasant Prefect' and wrote poetry in his honour. *The New York Times* and *The London Times* both effused about how Mori had 'broken the backbone of the Mafia', the former commenting on the 'spirit and resolution' of Mori and the manner by which he put himself in danger.

It will surprise many but for several years after the assumption of Fascism in 1922 there was no death penalty in Italy. The Fascist regime did not enact capital punishment until after the fourth attempt on Mussolini's life, and then only for treason, espionage and attempted assassination. Hence it might be surprising to realise that Mafiosi, even the many murderers, were not executed. Roger Eatwell, one of a few academics who have in recent years applied genuine scholarship to the study of Fascism, while stating that the methods employed against the Mafia were 'brutal', states that the number of sentences against the Mafia determined by the Special Tribunal for the Defence of the State between 1927 and 1939 was 3,596. The average sentence was

5.25 years imprisonment.[1] Neither figure seems exorbitant given what was achieved for Sicily and the extent of the brigandage decades.

Mori had been Prefect of Bologna prior to the Fascist regime. He was avid in quelling the civil unrest that prevailed on the streets between Socialists and Fascists. Ironically he was regarded as an enemy of the Fascist party, insisting on establishing order without fear or favour. In 1922, shortly before the Fascist assumption to Government, 20,000 Fascists converged on Bologna to demand Mori's resignation. He resisted, barricaded his police HQ, but was reassigned as Prefect of Bari, after which the civil disorder in Bologna between Socialists and Fascists intensified. In October the Fascists assumed Government. The following month Mori took early retirement and settled in Florence, assuming that his career was over.

Mussolini was determined to eliminate what had become a 'state within a state' in Sicily. In 1924 Mussolini went to Sicily and addressed a rapturous crowd, assuring them that the brigandage would be eliminated. Mori was called from retirement to return to Sicily and finish the job he had started in 1904. The local Fascisti looked with askance at the man who had shown no preferences in restoring order in Bologna, but Mori had been impressed already with the achievements of the regime and in particular a new spirit that was pervading Italy. He later wrote that the 'struggle with the Mafia had been fought to the finish for the first time under the Fascist regime'.

Mori knew Sicily and the Mafia well. Born in 1871, growing up in an orphanage, Mori studied at the Military academy in Turin, but entered the police and was sent to Sicily in 1904, where he first used his rigorous methods against the brigands. He was transferred to Florence in 1915 as assistant police chief. The world war saw a resurgence of the Mafia, and Mori was sent back to Sicily. However, Mori knew that the bandits he had arrested

---

1    Roger Eatwell, *Fascism: A History* (Vintage, 1996), 65-66.

by the hundreds were not the Mafia. Decorated for valour, he was sent to Turin, Rome and Bologna. Called out of retirement by the Fascist Government, Mori returned to Trapani, and was then appointed Perfect of Palermo, with jurisdiction over all of Sicily, a position he held until 1929, when he was appointed by Mussolini as a Senator. As Senator Mori continued to advocate for Sicily. He died in July 1942, precisely one year later the Allies landed on Sicily, and the Mafia heralded the way for 'Liberation'. Among the vanguard of democracy were Mafiosi who had returned from the USA with the invasion force.

Both the Sicilian Mafiosi and their American cousins could provide not only logistics for the Allies landing on Sicily, but could provide the manpower for the Occupation administration. U.S. Naval Intelligence was assigned to contact Mafiosi, with the assistance of the Jewish crime boss Meyer Lansky,[2] an ardent Zionist. Lansky states that he put Naval Intelligence in contact with Lucky Luciano, serving a lengthy jail sentence.[3]

Much has been written about Vito Genovese, the primary hit-man for Lucky Luciano. Genovese had fled the USA back to Italy to escape arrest. He is said to have ingratiated himself through donations to the Fascist party and to public works, with the Fascist regime, to the extent of becoming a close friend of Mussolini's and the supplier of cocaine to Mussolini's son-in-law and Foreign Minister Count Ciano. Yet Genovese became the most valuable Mafioso recruit for the Allied occupation, and had protectors in high places among the Allied military. Could this supposedly pro-Fascist Mafioso have been working for U.S. military intelligence since before the war, and was he permitted to escape trial for murder by leaving the USA for Italy in 1937? Robert Kelly et al state that Luciano used Genovese to alert the Mafia bosses to assist the Allied landing in Sicily.[4]

2   Timothy Newark, *The Mafia at War* (New York: Greenhill Books, 2007), 127.

3   Dennis Eisenberg, Uri Dan, Eli Landau, *Meyer Lansky: Mogul of the Mob* (New York: Paddington Press, 1979), 184-185.

4   Robert J. Kelly, Jess Maghan, Joseph Serio, *Illicit Trafficking: A Handbook* (Oxford:

# Introduction

With the Occupation of Italy Genovese became the primary advisor to the U.S. authorities, with high security clearance, and freedom of travel anywhere in Italy. It was only after the persistence of Sergeant Orange C. Dickey of the U.S. Army Criminal Investigation Department, who had uncovered the extensive black market empire of Genovese, that he was sent back to the USA to face charges, despite the high-level efforts to protect him. It seems that then the allegation was fostered that Genovese had been a Fascist sympathiser, to obscure his prominent role working for the U.S. Occupation.

Lansky states that he brought to Naval Intelligence and the OSS (forerunner of the CIA) 'hundreds of Sicilians' in the USA, who provided information on tides, beaches, roads and villages.[5]

The Mafia control of the waterfront unions in the USA, called Operation Underworld, had already been utilised to guard against possible Axis saboteurs on the docks. The *Normandie*, being used as a troop carrier, had been sunk at New York docks. The suspicion persists that it was the Mafia that sunk the ship then presented themselves as able to defend the docks from further sabotage. It was a replay of what their cousins and fathers had done for decades in Sicily: stealing livestock, then offering to find and return the property for a fee, often repeatedly.

Sicilians summoned to the office of Commander C. Radcliffe Haffenden of Naval Intelligence, who were reluctant to give information were warned that Lucky Luciano would not be pleased. Lansky suggested that Italian and Sicilian mobsters accompany the U.S. forces into Sicily as they would be best suited to obtain information. Portraying the Mafia as a version of Sherwood's 'Merry Men', loved by the poor, he said that they would be 'trusted' by Sicilians.[6] That this 'trust' and co-operation between Mafiosi and Sicilian folk would be based on fear had

---

ABC Clio, 2005), 129

5   Eisenberg, op. cit., 206.

6   Eisenberg, ibid., 208.

already been indicated by Lansky when he related that the threat of Luciano's name was enough to secure co-operation from Sicilians in the USA. With the Allied landing, Lansky states that the words 'Mafia' and 'Lucky Luciano' were virtual passwords to secure the co-operation of villagers.[7] Using Mafia contacts, U.S. Naval Intelligence agents were able to get 'key workers' in the ports of Sicily to keep the harbours operating to 'expedite the Allied landings', according to Lansky. The Mafia served as informants to the Allied Occupation government, identifying Fascists.[8] Lansky states that Allied commando units opened the prisons and released the Mafiosi and 'other anti-Fascist prisoners' and 'ordered', in the name of Luciano, them to serve as 'scouts and propagandists'. Mafiosi were appointed Mayors upon release from jail. Lansky states that the OSS reported that the Mafia had been crucial in the Allied landing. However, these 'Mafia heroes' soon established black markets, stealing Allied war supplies and pilfering scarce medicines to 'sell at high prices to the local peasants'.[9] Lansky states that Commander Haffenden told him that many of the members of Secret Intelligence Italy, staffed mainly by Sicilian-Americans who formed their own 'clique', were 'bitter' about the criticism of their methods.[10]

Among the first to greet the American tanks and jeeps was Don Calogero Vizzini, often referred to as the 'boss of bosses' of the Mafia. He boarded one of three American tanks and spent six days travelling through western Sicily, preparing the way for the American advance. This legend has been doubted, but seems credible given that he was made an Honorary Colonel of the U.S. Army. The U.S. occupiers installed him as Mayor of Villalba, while his Mafia deputy, Giuseppe Genco Russo, was appointed Mayor of the nearby village of Mussomeli.[11] The black

---

7    Eisenberg, ibid., 211.

8    Eisenberg, ibid., 213.

9    Eisenberg, ibid., 214.

10   Eisenberg, ibid., 215.

11   John Tagliabu, 'Villalba Journal: How Don Calo (and Patton) Won the War in Sicily', *New York Times*, 24 May 1994.

market empire established by Vinzzini throughout southern Italy was organised in partnership with Vito Genovese. In 1946 Luciano was pardoned in appreciation of his prominent role in assisting the Allied invasion of Sicily, and deported to Italy. In 1949 Vinzzini went into partnership with Luciano, establishing a 'candy factory' in Palermo as a front for manufacturing and distributing heroin throughout Europe, until exposed by *Avanti!* newspaper in 1954. Portrayed as a Robin Hood type figure, he had obtained his wealth, like many other brigands, through cattle, horse and mule rustling, and extortion, during World War I, and taking hefty tracts of land from the peasants while posing as a champion of land reform.

Sicily was soon back to the brigandage that had stunted Sicily for generations prior to Mori. The Italian State was now expending much more against the Mafia than Mori had, with 8,000 heavily armed *carabinieri* spending four years from 1946 attempting to suppress the most notorious, Salvatore Giuliani's small band, although he was courted by politicians of the Christian Democrat and Liberal parties who sought Mafia support. The Mafia, which had prior to Fascism held political sway in Sicily, placed their allegiance with the Christian Democrats, the preferred party of the 'Liberation', when it became apparent that Sicilian separatism, supported by Giulian, was abortive. The party governed and shaped Italy for most of the post-war era, until imploding in 1994 through corruption scandals that included Mafia associations.

Kerry Bolton

# The Last Struggle
# With
# The Mafia

# Part One

## The Mafia In Pre-Fascist Days

### The Problem Of Public Safety In Sicily

There has been an unnecessary amount of talk about the so-called problem of public safety in Sicily. In form and in fact this problem presented itself as such owing to the joint occurrence of three phenomena *plus* an unknown quantity. The three phenomena, briefly, were these:—

1. *A predominant activity of crime,* which was serious owing to the number and quality of the crimes of every kind committed, with a growing prevalence of specific and endemic forms of crime (homicide, robbery, blackmail, cattle-stealing, association for criminal purposes), to the evil infection of every branch of social activity and to the resultant stagnation of the country's productive energies;

2. *The chronic failure of State action* in its fight against crime in the island;

3. *The rapidly increasing tendency of the people to hold aloof and wrap themselves in such reserve* as to render investigation impossible.

The unknown quantity was the Mafia—a specific local element of which I shall speak in the sequel.

What was the situation? It has often been described, but undoubtedly the most authoritative and objective reflection of it is to be found in the annual reports made by the King's Procurator-General of the Sicilian Court of Appeal —especially in the court at Palermo—at the opening of the judicial year.

These exact and carefully drawn up accounts, although one may sometimes disagree with their statement of causes and remedies, cannot be impugned as regards the statement of fact. I shall restrict myself to quoting the last of these, the report read by the King's Procurator-General of Palermo, on January 19th, 1931, in which His Excellency, who had put all the strength of his faith, intellect, and good sense into the fight against the Mafia, expressed himself in the following terms:

"What were the conditions of the district in 1925 is known to all. The Mafia dominated and controlled the whole social life, it had leaders and followers, it issued orders and decrees, it was to be found equally in big cities and in small centres, in factories and in rural districts, it regulated agricultural and urban rents, forced itself into every kind of business, and got its way by means of threats and intimidation or of penalties imposed by its leaders and put into execution by its officers. Its orders had the force of laws and its protection was a legal protection, more effective and secure than that which the State offers to its citizens; so that owners of property and business men insured their goods and their persons by submitting to pay the price of the insurance. A man who was travelling by night, or even by day, in some parts of Sicily, did better to be accompanied by two associates of the Mafia than by two or more members of the police force.[1]

"Thus property and persons were secure. The associations of the small centres ordinarily exercised jurisdiction in them, or in the adjoining communes: those of the more important centres were in communication with one another and with those in adjacent provinces, and lent one another mutual assistance. It not infrequently occurred that in the same commune there were two Mafias, either deliberately created, spontaneously generated or born of some dispute over the booty, contending for supremacy. The result of this was a bitter struggle involving the deaths of

---

1    Translator's Note.—Here and throughout I translate, for convenience, *la forza pubblica* by "police." Strictly speaking, the Italian phrase connotes the *Carabinieri*, an independent Corps, and other occasional forces as well.

leaders and more influential members of the executive and of their respective families: and the mortal conflict would continue for generations till whole families had been extinguished. . . .

"As the strong oak spreads its branches and produces a fruitful crop of acorns, so the Mafia associations, by means of their members and under the careful but hidden direction of their leaders, carried out the criminal actions from which they reaped the advantage of their criminal bond and by which they were able to keep their domination respected and feared. Hence the increase in the district of murders, robberies, blackmail, kidnapping, private violence and injurious actions both quantitatively and qualitatively deplorable in that they bore upon them the terrible imprint of the terrible association.

"Murder was committed when a man would not obey the order to allow himself to be robbed or to send the money demanded either in threatening letters or after the kidnapping of some member of the family, or to wreak the Mafia's vengeance for similar offences, or as a result of other serious disobediences or lapses, of which the chief was that of violating the law of *omertà*—the law of silence with regard to the criminal actions of the Mafia.

"Murder was the expression of vengeance to be carried out at all costs, at whatever risk, if risk there was in some cases of great importance. It was either to be wrought on the person inculpated—direct vengeance—or against other members of the family or of the association—indirect vengeance—and barbarously, savagely, by surprise, by ambush, with stones, with razors, with scythes, with guns, by poisoning, by beheading, by strangling and then dishonouring the corpse, by soaking with paraffin and then setting alight, or by mutilation or horrible disfigurement as a mark of the terrifying power of the Mafia.

"Robbery was not of the usual kind in which the wayfarer, threatened with a weapon, is forced to give up some article he is carrying. It was the typical, classical highway-robbery, carried out by several persons, usually armed with guns and clothed in hooded mantles or ample overcoats, with their heads covered, and their eyes hidden by smoked spectacles or by handkerchiefs with two holes in them for the eyes. Guns were levelled, the order 'face to the ground' was given, and those who disobeyed were killed, while the rest were robbed of their possessions or were bound and taken elsewhere while some of the highwaymen carried off the booty they had captured. Not seldom robbery assumed vast proportions, either through the number of the robbers or through the quantity of the objects to be robbed, such as mules, horses, grain, cattle, and sometimes whole herds of small or large beasts. These depredations sometimes led to pitched battles when their object was a farmstead and the robbers were the armed bands which especially infested this province and that of Agrigento.

"Blackmail also assumed an unusual form, since it was hardly ever due to the action of a single individual, but to that of the association for whose profit, or for that of its chiefs or of persons pre-eminent in it, the crime was committed by its members. A first, a second, and then a third request to deposit money in a fixed place would be issued, with a threat of grave injury usually expressed by a cross, a skull, or a dagger; and when the written threat did not achieve its aim, other more effective warnings followed—arson, damage to property, the cutting down of vines or trees and, in the last resort, personal injury or the kidnapping of a child or other member of the family. Besides this form of direct, open blackmail, there were other silent and not less effective forms, expressed as requests for money to secure mediation or other services, not accompanied by verbal or symbolic threats, but by real threats made personally by the blackmailer or inferred from the fact that the person making the demand belonged to the Mafia.

"No less frequent or remarkable were the instances of kidnapping in which, a person having been kidnapped for the purpose of extorting money, the ransom was sometimes so exorbitant as to deprive the sufferer of the greater part, if not of the whole, of his property. He, as may well be supposed, was compelled to submit, for if he delayed to pay, or did not pay, the sum demanded, he was answered by receiving the corpse of the kidnapped person bearing the terrible marks of vengeance and punishment.

"You cannot get the faintest idea of the crimes committed by the Mafia in past times without having read in the records of trials in which the large or small associations were involved, of the murders, the depredations, the incendiarism, the violence, the rapes, the savage and atrocious vengeances committed by members of these ill-famed associations; without having lived the life of those days and having seen the acts of homicide, the robberies, and the acts of violence committed by day, in broad daylight, even in the public streets of Palermo, the dead lying on the ground, the murderers in safety; without having been a victim of the brigand bands which infested towns and countryside— the bands of the Andaloros, the Ferrarellos, the Dinos, and the Saccos—spreading everywhere terror, slaughter and violence.

"Indeed, the serious prevalence of crime is shown by the figures relative to robbery, blackmail and kidnapping, of which the cases in 1922 were 2,365, in 1923 were 1,960, and in 1924 were 1,768: and it must be borne in mind that these figures do not represent the real total, since a greater part of the crimes were not denounced for fear of reprisals on the part of their authors."

That was the situation, an undeniably grave one but, as I have said, extremely clear.

# Some Theories

The prevalence of crime in Sicily naturally caused great anxiety: the causes and the possible remedies were studied by many. Some profound works by men of intellect and science bear witness to these researches in the field of thought, as, in the field of action, tragic crosses bear witness to the silent heroism of many who lost their lives at the call of duty. Some of the theorisers, it has been observed, lost themselves in a tangle of inconclusive commonplaces: but certain other theories, though less inconclusive, were more dangerous or, to say the least, less disinterested. Some of them, therefore, are not without interest.

One theory, to begin with, was simplicity itself. It denied, not only the grave problem of public security, but any specifically criminal quality in the Mafia, regarding it as indistinguishable from the type of criminal agency common to all countries. Some people even went so far as to invent the slogan: "The Mafia? . . . Why Mori invented it!" The conclusion from this total negative was that there was nothing to be done, and that the desire to do anything was a libel on Sicily. Probably people would still have been talking in this way if, at an opportune moment, the *Duce* had not intervened with the stern words:

> "From time to time there come to my ears doubting voices that wish to suggest that today we are going too far in Sicily, that an entire region is being harshly treated and that a slur is being cast over an island of the noblest traditions. I reject with utter contempt these suggestions which can only originate from persons of evil reputation."[2]

---

2    From a speech made to the Chamber of Deputies on May 20th, 1927.

Another strange theory, also negative, was one which, leaving the character of the Mafia and of the criminality of the island on one side, denied the existence of a problem on different grounds. It was contended that the absence of social uneasiness, shown by the mute and indifferent attitude of the populace, gave reasons for supposing that, by a gradual process of adaptation, the populace itself had become habituated to the existing moral climate. The upholders of this theory urged that nothing should, or could, be done; that the best thing in such cases was inaction; that all should be left to time; that outside intervention would disturb the natural biological process which would irresistibly end in one of two things—either the populace would absorb the criminals, or (and here was the catch) the criminals would absorb the populace. And that is not all. There were also the peacemakers who refused to admit a problem, or only saw, or pretended to see, the harshness of the struggle in which the forces of the State, albeit spasmodically, occasionally, and with ill-fortune, but with undoubted personal courage, were fighting for the defence of society. There were all kinds of peacemakers and they all talked of making peace; but between whom was peace to be made? Between the opposing sides, of course: that is, between the evildoers on one side and the authorities and populace on the other. There was nothing very extraordinary in this: it simply meant the nullification of the problem of public safety by means of conciliation.

And there was another type of peacemaking, that by *détente*. When, as sometimes happened, the State threatened to act decisively and, when success, even temporary, seemed to be at hand, then the thousand voices, known and unknown, of the Mafia, sent out the S.O.S., which was caught up by friends and protectors and launched to the four winds. The cry went up: "Things are going too far in Sicily!" It was a clumsy but effective manoeuvre; for it was always carried out at the right moment, when public opinion had been made particularly susceptible to gloomy forebodings by some succession of serious incidents. Then there would ensue the so-called pacific intervention, involving, of course, a slackening of the pressure. Thereupon, the shipwrecked mariners of the Mafia, all but drowned, came to the surface again, quiet and silent for the moment. There was a sensation of ephemeral truce, naturally: but this did not prevent them beginning again at the first opportunity. And the first opportunity, of course, was never wanting! Such was the so-called pacification which, whatever form it took, implied in substance the idea of *"après nous le déluge!"* And the deluge always came.

Not that I am against pacification. Quite the contrary. But the only peace for me is a true peace, not a parody of peace or a grotesque temporary expedient based on doubtful grounds of policy, attained by acquiescence and compromise and of an efficacy as limited as the horizon of the opportunists. The peace that I have in mind can only be attained by assuring to the individual and to the mass—especially to those in a state of social inferiority—the indispensable minimum of security below which, too often, honesty is apt to seem vain heroism.

The most prevalent theories, however, were two in number and had a common point of departure. Both recognised specific racial and politico-sociological factors in the situation. The first laid stress on the exuberance, impulsiveness and passion of the Sicilian temperament—qualities easily perverted to become the springs and inspirations of criminal action. The second laid stress on the unsatisfactory economic, social and political conditions under which Sicily had so long laboured: illiteracy, pauperism, landlordism, malaria, urban overcrowding, economic subjection, patronage, interference in elections and persistent neglect, they said, were the real causes of crime by weakening resistance to temptation.

The first, therefore, regarded the problem chiefly as one of police action against peculiarly aggressive criminals aided by a general quasi-complicity on the part of the people: while the second regarded it as a result of economic and social depression which could only be treated on social-economic lines as an integral part of the complex question of southern Italy. The first looked on the problem as specifically a Sicilian one, the second as one involved in far wider issues. It was natural, then, that the first should see the solution in direct and immediate police measures, and the second should see it in the improvement of economic, social and political conditions.

Both, although in perfect good faith and logical consistency, erred—the first from shortsightedness, the second from longsightedness. Probably the truth lay between the two, as men say that it always does. In fact, admitting that the problem was properly stated by these two currents of opinion—on which point I make some reserves—the logical solution could only come from the harmonious fusion of the two points of view: that is to say, in police action and in thoroughgoing social-economic intervention carried out simultaneously, in harmonious combination and above all, at a reasonable pace, with particular attention to the opportune moment for action. Moreover, the slower and more distant in action the social-economic intervention, the more rapid and continuous would the development of police action have to be, not only as an end in itself, but as a means of creating and maintaining all the material, spiritual and psychological conditions necessary for the application and absorption of social-economic measures.

# Reaching The Heart Of A People

The government's chronic failure to repress crime, and the mutual mistrust that arose between the people and the authorities, brought matters to a standstill. Nothing was done, and all hope of doing anything seemed lost. Many dismissed the problem from their minds as too painful to think of, and others lost all perspective, hypnotised by the accounts of sanguinary encounters that they read in the police reports. But there were some, like myself, who saw that the only means of arriving at the truth was to live among the people and penetrate the mystery of sorrow and silence that wrapped the desolate countryside. This I did. I got to know them all, the good and the bad, the weak and the strong, the humble and the proud, sharing their faith, their emotions, their sorrows and their hopes, and adapting myself to their many ways of self-expression, their habits and their necessities, and even to their outward characteristics, till I almost became one of them.

Of this I have some amusing memories. There were, for instance, some *latitanti*[3] who, many years ago, were harrying one of the districts of the island and being hotly pursued. I was personally engaged in drawing the net closer round them; and one of them had already lost his life. One day they came to a lawyer in the chief town—he told me the story later with a smile of amusement—to put their case to him, but first broke into violent abuse and bellicose threats against me, until the oldest of them silenced them by saying:—

*"Zittitivi: l'aviti a rispittare; chiddu è omo ca ci la sape a fari lu latitanti megghiu assai di nuautri.* (Shut up; you ought to respect

---
3   Fugitives from justice.

25

him; he's a man who can play the *latitante* better than any of us.)

That was an honorary diploma in *latitanza* which may raise a smile, but which, looked at seriously, especially where it approaches the feeling of respect, gives food for thought.

And these unhappy men were not entirely wrong, for more than once I was taken for a *latitante*, with amusing consequences. One day, for instance, while I was riding through a wood with a police agent, I encountered a harmless soldier of the Red Cross who was going round distributing quinine. This man, when he came within ten paces of me, and without my making any motion, fell on his knees on one side of the path, begging for mercy and swearing that he had not a halfpenny on him. We had a hard job to reassure him, and it needed a drop of brandy to put him on his legs again.

"Listen, sir," said the police agent to me a little later, "let us shave at least, for something inside me tells me that, in our present state, we shall be exchanging shots before night—but not with the bad men."

His prophecy almost came true. Half an hour later we came out of the wood in front of a clearing. A hundred yards farther on there was a threshing floor where threshing was going on busily, and I noticed that, on our appearing, the farmer, retiring cautiously behind a heap of sheaves, unslung his double-barrelled gun from his shoulder and quickly changed the cartridges. Only our indifferent demeanour kept him puzzled, until, on our coming up to him, the misunderstanding was cleared up. However, the fact was that he had substituted two cartridges containing bullets surrounded by small shot for cartridges of small shot only.

And this kind of thing did not happen in the country districts alone. Several years ago it happened that I had to rush in a great hurry from the hills to Palermo. I was wearing very rustic clothes and did not wish to attract attention, for which reason I went to a very modest inn to pass the night. I had the usual police agent with me, and his appearance, I admit, was not particularly reassuring. It was late on a winter's evening. Our appearance at the top of the steps of the inn did not rouse excessive enthusiasm. We were evidently mistaken for two *persecuti*[4] and were taken into a little room apart and left alone, with the timid warning that neither food nor beds could be provided, in the vain hope, no doubt, that we should go away.

Seeing what was up, I cheerfully took up the *rôle* assigned to me. I gave imperious orders for supper, and while the wan waiter, who had certainly been given orders to be obstructive, came in and out cautiously to lay the table, I began to talk with my companion of our affairs, ... like a real bandit in an expansive mood: and I told dreadful tales enough to make the hair stand up on the plaster bust of an unknown person that was frowningly decorating an empty side-table. So long as I only spoke of blackmail and robbery under arms the supper served by that poor devil of a waiter remained scanty. But when, as a last resort, I came out with a murder, pretending to happy recollections of the victim's terrible cries, the wan waiter was seen no more and the meal, served very obsequiously by the landlord himself, became worthy of Lucullus. Not only that, but we were given comfortable beds and almost motherly care.

In the morning early, a cart, whose driver had of course been given the tip by the landlord, took us to our destination by back ways so remote that I had never dreamed of their existence. As for payment: *"Ma che dice vossia!"* (Don't mention it, your honour!) the landlord exclaimed when I asked for the bill. I had a hard struggle to pay at all, for the landlord and the waiter were vying for the privilege of paying for us themselves.

Another amusing episode: I had been beating certain high ground in the interior of the island which was said to be a favourite hiding place of a group of *latitanti* at whose door

---

4    Men wanted by the police.

some serious crimes were laid. It was a rough, almost savage, existence, because the necessities of our task made us keep entirely away from all habitations. However, one morning at dawn, my men having gone off on some duty or other, I went up to a little cottage that looked clean, in the hope of finding some refreshment there. I was alone, dressed like a rustic and mounted on a shaggy horse, armed and pretty dirty—a sort of knight of the rueful countenance. A kind-looking old woman received me with obvious signs of anxiety.

"Can you give me a lemon?" I asked in dialect.

No answer.

The old woman looked at me for a little and then said: "Are you going about like this? Think of your mother. Don't you know he is going round these parts?"

"No, I don't. Whom do you mean?"

*"Iddu."* (Him.)

*"Him?* Who?"

"Mori!"

"Good heavens! Thanks, good woman," I went on, "but if you'll give me a lemon you'll do me a still greater service."

And so she did. A little later on, as I was sitting outside the door of the cottage, two of my men came up to tell me what they had been doing. Tableau! The old woman, who was looking at us, suddenly had a revelation: she understood.

*"Bedda matri! Iddu è!"* (Holy Mother, it's him!) she exclaimed.

I shall never forget the horrified expression on her face. But it was only for a moment: for then, coming up to me with one of those simple gestures of the hands which only the humble know how to make, she added with emotion: *"Tutto buono e biniritto, ma guardatevi!"* (Bless you, sir, but be on your guard!)

*Iddu è!* How often I heard this exclamation, and how often it was made even when I was not there! *Iddu* è! Popular fancy almost created round that phrase a figure endowed with magical gifts, present everywhere and at all times in the most varied shapes and able to read anybody's mind like an open book. I could tell many stories on that subject, but will content myself with a few.

In one of the centres in the interior most infested with evildoers the police under my control had succeeded by a fortunate operation in capturing a number of dangerous persons, among whom was a redoubtable *latitante* accused of serious crimes and the notorious head of a criminal association. So far all was well. The difficulties began when the question arose of bringing concrete proof of the guilt of the arrested men. The neighbourhood, terrorised by the long unpunished acts of the criminals, remained mute and aloof. Those who had suffered threats, robberies, thefts, blackmail and worse, resigned to their losses and their griefs, discouraged and terrified by the prospect of eventual reprisals, kept silence, denied or did not remember. The accused, on their side, merrily lied or manifested extreme surprise. The chief, cool, impassive and brazen, persisted stubbornly in answering questions with short, sharp monosyllables of negation such as to discourage the cleverest investigator. In these circumstances the stroke threatened to fail for want of proof.

It was already night, and a decision had to be come to. It was then that a young official made an experiment. Taking one of the headlights of the lorry which served as the police transport and disguising it with a cloth, he directed its beam upon the *latitante*, around whom there was now a pall of darkness and silence, and said to him in a solemn tone :—

"You have asked for it: now you will *have* to speak: denial is useless. Look, this is Mori's eye, and it can see right down into your soul."

Absurd! Incredible! But the fact remains that, whether from dismay or suggestion, the *latitante* confronted with that eye spoke and confessed his crime.

Here is another very amusing instance—the last that I experienced. A few days before I definitely gave up my office, near a village in the vicinity of Palermo, two criminals were going along a country road, driving two mules they had stolen a little earlier. Suddenly, at a turn in the road, their eyes fell on a monk sitting quietly on the parapet of a bridge. The two fellows looked at one another with questioning glances. The monk had the most peaceable look in the world: but . . . it was said that, among other things, I used to disguise myself as a monk. Indeed, some people swore that they had seen me going about in that costume, as lonely and silent as a ghost, in the most closely ambushed quarters. Anyhow, our two friends did not feel easy. They went on for a few stumbling steps, and then the same thought occurred to both of them, the same words leapt to their lips: *Iddu* è! So, abandoning the stolen mules, they took to their heels, to the high glee of a peasant who secured the two animals and led them away to tell of the little scene.

For my own part I simply reflect how much truth is contained in the old Sicilian proverb: *fatti la fama e cúrcati.* The literal translation is "get a reputation and go to bed," but it means, "to get yourself known is enough." But you must get known, of course, by actions: and at the same time you must get to know; and this by direct, immediate personal contacts, in which the hearts not only of individuals, but of the people at large, reveal themselves completely, without disguise, in ways that are unexpected and often very moving.

My first experience of this occurred in that proud and generous country to which I am linked by fond and imperishable memories of youth—I mean Romagna. I speak of several years ago, when I was a police official at Ravenna during a period of some excitement. The central problem was the chronic excess of labour. Unemployment, very appreciable at all seasons, became grievously aggravated during the winter. Several thousand strong and healthy men, well known to be hearty workers and specialists in digging the ground, found themselves and their families condemned to absolute inertia, and in the greatest distress at the most inclement season of the year. They had no resources and no reserves: the little work they had had during the year had not allowed them to collect any. Their only capital was their arms, their spades and their wheelbarrows—all condemned to idleness.

They held out as long as they could: and then, little by little, they descended in a mass on Ravenna in a demonstrative attitude to give the authorities tangible proof of the state things had reached. The authorities, on their part, tried to provide for them, as far as they could, with public works. Nothing serious took place; at the same time, these descents of unemployed labourers *en masse* always caused anxiety, for which reason orders were given to stop the various groups outside the city gates and only to allow deputations of varying numbers to enter. Usually matters ended in that way. Once, however, alarming warnings reached us from the countryside. A descent *en masse* of all the unemployed labourers had been announced for the following morning. The men's state of mind was known to be irritable and many of them had been breathing threats of violence. I was told to go out the same night on reconnaisance to ascertain and report the size and character of the movement in good time so that adequate measures could be taken and the approaches to the town be blocked in time. I left the town amid snow and fog with five cyclists and made at once for the most distant villages. All night long I came on clubs, league headquarters, union offices and *cameracce* (a kind of club-inn) open and packed with rather excited labourers. I spoke with many of them, I discussed and argued: all was useless. At dawn the movement on Ravenna began. As soon as I had ascertained the size of a party and its line of march, I sent off a cyclist to Ravenna with the requisite information. When the last of my five cyclists had gone, I had one more road to examine. I went alone and, as I was going along it, I met a strong group of labourers which came from one of the most turbulent parts of the commune. Getting off my bicycle, I asked the group to stop. The demonstrators stopped. But when I pointed out the uselessness of their descent on Ravenna—especially with the intentions that they had—and warned them that they would find the bridges blocked by the police, the crowd gave lively signs of impatience and threatened to go on. I tried again, putting the case once more in such forcible words that there was a moment of halt and a threatening silence. The situation was obviously taking an ugly turn. But just at that moment, one of the most violent ringleaders, in calm, cordial and meaning tone said to me: "You only talk like that because you're alone!"

All the heart of a Romagnole was in those words. I need not say that the situation immediately became brighter. We each went our own ways, and two hours later we met again, I at the head of the troop who were blocking a bridge, they with their body of comrades. There was no clash, no incident, no bad results. Not only that: but in a short space of time, in spite of—and perhaps because of—the resolute attitude which my duty, in those agitated times, often obliged me to take up, the personal contact and the reciprocal understanding that began that morning increased and became warmed with good feeling. And a day came when, with profound emotion, I heard those very Romagnole labourers, to whom in the name of the law and order I had so often had to bar the way, singing the following refrain:

*Sa passu da què Mori, à vlém, andèr con ló.* (If Mori comes this way, we want to go with him.)

# Gleams Of Light

The stories I told in the last chapter are minor episodes and their characters are sketchy; but they explain clearly how I was able to penetrate the Sicilian mind. I found this mind, beneath the painful scars with which centuries of tyranny and oppression had marked it, often childlike, simple and kindly, apt to colour everything with generous feeling, ever inclined to deceive itself, to hope and to believe, and ready to lay all its knowledge, its affection and its co-operation at the feet of one who showed a desire to realise the people's legitimate dream of justice and redemption. To the timid, therefore, it remained a closed book: but it is open to be read by all men except those whose hearts have become hardened by the continual perusal of police records or who have become obsessed by the statistics of crime. To such as these I specially dedicate the episodes and sketches of living people that follow.

To begin with, here is a little shepherd boy, a ragged, weedy, dark lad, with great, precociously thoughtful eyes, whom I met on a far-off, gloomy autumn afternoon, standing motionless in his stiff waterproof under the lash of the rain and the wind, alone in the dreary solitude of a vast and ill-famed prairie. In silent resignation, he was guarding a flock of sheep. He moved me to pity. I got off my horse and talked to him for some time. And he talked too. And thus it was that, from the lips of a child, of an innocent boy, in an hour of melancholy and solitude, I had my first revelation. His father? Wanted by the police, and in America. His mother? Sick and alone in the village with two small children. His village? Far off. How far? He did not know, for he never went there. God, prayer, school? He knew nothing about such things. The King, Italy, his fatherland? Nothing, either. The law, duty, right and wrong, good and bad? Nothing again. Men? Sheep were better than men, he said, because the only men he had seen so far were either evildoers who beat him to make him submit to be robbed, or his master who beat him to make him tell how many sheep had been stolen, or the police who wanted him to tell them things that he neither knew nor understood. And he looked at me, that little shepherd boy, from under his stiff waterproof hood, with a mute questioning look to which I found no answer.

Here is another. A man this time, a *latitante*, guilty of murder and for some time vainly tracked by the police. A legend of invulnerability had formed round him which included his wife, who was reputed to be his watchful, tigerish, fearless companion. For the authorities, therefore, his capture was a question of prestige. One day I broke into his house by surprise. It was dinner-time. Round the poor table sat the wife and five children: in their midst an empty place, a chair on the ground, a still smoking plate. The *latitante* had just had time to jump out of the window, leaving his gun behind. On my appearing, while the children burst out crying, the wife got up ready to defend her man and tell the most devoted lies. To her, who had the reputation of being a virago, I spoke as one ought to speak to a mother and a wife; and I went away leaving on that unhappy table a small coin to be spent on the children. Three days later the elusive *latitante* came to see me in my office, and the only answer that he made to my questions was to kiss my hand and weep.

Here is another—a woman, of the lowest class, absolutely primitive and therefore subject to the tradition of such families that the woman should be blindly obedient to her husband and always show him respect. Her husband was quite a common criminal who had succeeded by his own efforts in making a certain point on the provincial main road near the town a danger spot. In the hours of dusk, behind the hedges on each side of the road he would rig two old *scapolari* (overcoats with hoods) on sticks to give them the look of men in ambush armed with guns, and he himself, armed with an old, empty blunderbuss, would shout to passers-by "Face to the ground!" They, in the growing darkness, thinking that he was supported by the two shapes behind the hedges, would hold up their hands and allow themselves to be robbed without ado. The wife, who was worried and annoyed by these goings-on, of which she was aware, had often timidly tried to persuade her husband to give them up and take to honest work. But it had been quite useless. At last, one evening, seeing her husband making ready to leave their hovel for his usual expedition, the poor woman—who had already decided what she would do—renewed her insistence, adding: "Mind, something tells me it will go badly this time." The man only gave a grunt and, taking his two old overcoats and the rusty blunderbuss, went out.

It was already growing dark. The woman gave a glance at the dark sky and then, hastily pulling on a pair of trousers, wrapping herself in an old blanket and arming herself with a broom-handle, she hurried down a steep short-cut which came out a kilometre further on into the road by which her unwitting husband was going. And there she lay in wait. A few minutes later, when her husband reached the spot, he saw a shadow rise out of the gloom and point a hazy but menacing weapon at his chest, while a gruff voice shouted to him: "*A terra!*" Our friend, with a quick sad glance at the two overcoats that hung flapping on his arm and with a melancholy thought of the empty blunderbuss slung on his shoulder, felt a cold shiver run down his spine, threw himself on the ground without a murmur, and recommended himself to God's mercy, remembering how many had done the same thing at his command. The shadow came up stealthily. It bound him firmly, in the proper way, his hands behind his back: it tied his feet, too, and then, while the man's teeth were chattering in the expectation of the avenging charge of small shot that would settle his business, a tempest of cudgel blows fell upon him and made all his bones rattle without any heed to his long-drawn moans. How long it continued he never knew; but the fact remains that when, about an hour later, he was able to untie himself and make his way home, sorry and beaten and aching all over, his wife, poor soul, who was awaiting him with obvious anxiety and affectionately bathed with vinegar and water the bumps left on his head by the very unheroic adventure, said to him in honeyed tones: "Didn't I tell you I had a presentiment?" And from that time onwards, thanks to a wretched woman, the fields of that district had one worker more, and the high road one danger less.

Here is another. A youth this time, broken to every vice, violent, cynical and completely gone to the bad. Having been arrested one day on somewhat general grounds for complicity in a serious crime, he stoutly maintained his innocence, alleging one of the usual *alibis*. Suddenly, three days later, while his *alibi* was gaining in consistency, he confessed his guilt. I asked to speak to him myself. We had a long skirmish, but finally he gave up. "I am twenty-one," he said, "and I have no family responsibilities. Perhaps they won't condemn me. But if they do, what are six or seven years' prison to me? Meanwhile, my confession clears that other poor chap (he alluded to another prisoner) who is almost an old man and has a family dying of hunger." And that was true.

Here is another episode. Several years ago, when I was busily engaged in hunting down a dangerous armed band which was acting in three adjacent provinces of the island, I was obliged, in the absence of a motor car, to save time and horses by availing myself pretty frequently of the railway. They were long and tiresome journeys, but I had already acquired the habit of getting a good sleep in the train, which refreshed me after the discomforts of my very active duties. One day, as I was waiting for one of the ordinary trains on the platform of the railway station of C. and was looking forward to the pleasure of a quiet nap, I saw a rather sinister figure of the locality bend a glance of expressive insistence on me. He was a Mafia chief, well-known, feared and intimately associated with bandits and *latitanti*, whom I myself had had arrested and tried three times in the course of a few years. I went towards him slowly, and when I came up to him I took out a cigarette and asked him for a match.

He respectfully took a box of matches out of his pocket and, as he gave it me, he whispered: *"Voscienza un ave a dòrmere chiù in treno"* (Your Honour shouldn't go to sleep in trains any more.) I said good-bye to him and departed; but I heeded the warning, and I found out that the armed band I was hunting was plotting to surprise me in my sleep as I travelled in the very first tunnel after C. Some time later, having captured the band, I left Sicily for another destination. While talking to some friends who had come to say good-bye to me as I passed through C, I saw my Mafia chief sitting all alone in a corner of the station and silently weeping as he gazed at me.

One more figure: the last. This one is a real brigand, solitary and fierce, accustomed to blood and booty, a hardened criminal, a stranger to pity, brutal in appearance, burdened with a sinister and bloody reputation that made everyone afraid of him, with a heavy price on his head and hunted incessantly like a wild beast. One night the police surprised and surrounded him in a hut hidden among the olive trees. He was alone; he shut himself in, bolted the door and began to shoot. It was a tragic battle, for he seemed to have a cat's eyes and to see in the dark. And his shooting was very accurate. All at once one of the police was hit and fell with a groan at the foot of an olive tree. The bandit observed it and fired more heavily at that spot. In the growing darkness those who were nearest the fallen man, heedless of their own safety, approached to carry him away. One of them whispered: "Keep low, and don't bunch." Then, in a moment of silence such as sometimes occurs in the midst of a storm, a voice was heard in the night; it was the voice of the bandit saying: "I'll stop firing; take your comrade away." And he stopped firing till the sorry group over which death was already spreading her wings had moved off. The battle started again and, at break of dawn, the man was overcome and forced to surrender. I saw him a few hours later, handcuffed and sullen, marching towards his sad fate. I scrutinised his face and tried to see into his heart. It was impenetrable.

Yet from this episode, as from the others and from many more that I could tell, unexpected gleams of light lit up the tragic picture of Sicilian crime—gleams that showed the active presence of a powerful but imponderable influence, a property of the Sicilian race. The presence of this influence, which could inspire almost or entirely lost men to fleeting but unmistakable marks of better feeling, really undermined the whole condemnatory structure which had been too easily, and at Sicily's sole expense, built on the three fatal words: Mafia, crime and *omertà*. With these things we must now get a closer acquaintance.

# Omertà

I cannot say exactly from what this word originates. Probably from the Latin word *homo* (man). Indeed, some people hold that it was originally *omineità*. Anyhow—although many people will not believe it—omertà is certainly not an exclusive property of any place or country. *Omertà* began with man, and is a cosmopolitan, universal fact. The word itself has two meanings—the primitive and the present.

In its primitive meaning the word *omertà* covers all individual expressions of vigorous and healthy manliness, in the loftiest sense of that term, as in phrases like: "He is a real man," or more simply: "He's a *man*" In Sicily the article is suppressed and they say; "He is man," or sometimes *"Quello è màsculu"* (male). Manliness in this sense, in all places and times, has a constant connotation which is complete self-confidence, a high sense of honour, duty and personal dignity, a gallant heart, a balanced judgment and self-control. Pure *omertà* refers to men of this kind; and it is a form of aristocracy of character in this primitive meaning, derived from a high conception of healthy, masculine energies.

A special characteristic of *omertà* is reserve, a quality which found its most significant expression in the silence generally implicit in the meaning of the word. It is a noble silence, proud and stoical, not to be confused with the silence of the proverb: "Silence is golden"; with the prudential silence of the saying: "Unspoken words cannot be recorded"; or with the silence of fear which often changes into an absurd volubility. The silence I speak of is a silence compatible with aristocracy of character.

Omertà

In its original meaning *omertà* also implies exemption from the common law: as such it embodies the pride of all rebels against injustice and tyranny, in every age and country, besides a particular view of questions involving personal honour. It is easy to understand, then, that *omerta*, in its original sense, has always exerted a special influence over the masses, for the masses love the man who can take the law into his own hands to revenge an injury better than him who can forgive.

*Omertà* would, therefore, particularly tend to flourish in a country like Sicily where the spirit of pride and individuality is most lively and insistent, where justice and social protection were most seriously deficient, and where the chief source of injustice and tyranny was the government itself. It would tend to be looked on as a noble quality, issue in acts of reprisal and work against the government. This, in fact, was what happened.

The consequences were that the whole people, being victims of tyranny and oppression, became affected, thus producing a peculiar form of local *omertà*, shown chiefly in the protection of rebels and refusal to give evidence against them; and further, that associations for self-defence against oppression, bound together by the caste-spirit of *omertà*, were formed among the people. These associations, such as the sect of the Beati Paoli, described by Vincenzo Linares in his *Racconti Popolari* (Palermo, 1886), although born of a natural impulse to self-defence, inevitably tended to degenerate. Their original ends were perverted and their violent actions made them a danger to society.

There are other, and more or less perverted forms of *omertà*. There is, for instance, a purely selfish form shown by energetic, self-willed and possibly quite respectable individuals in taking the law into their own hands, regardless of the consequences to other people. This form of *omertà* would not be very important if it did not result in a very dangerous attitude. The man who says: "So long as nobody crosses me, I don't care what anybody else does, and I don't want to know" is a danger to the common weal, because evildoers readily adapt themselves to this attitude, thinking in their turn: "All right; I won't touch you, but I'll make up for it on the others: and all the easier for being able to count on your disregard of what happens to others and on your consequent silence." This implied immunity on reciprocal terms is an obvious danger to the community.

Another perverted form is *compulsory omertà*. This arises where and when the unrestricted spread of crime has forced respectable people into compromises and arrangements with criminals which, in return for their own immunity from violence, enforce acquiescence and silence upon them. Of this passive form of *omertà*, enforced upon entire districts by criminals, I shall have more to say later.

As a matter of fact, the advance of civilisation and the greater efficiency of the law, together with the power of public opinion, have deprived *omertà* in its original sense of any further reason for existence.

The very word has fallen into disuse, but the conception has lingered in the tendency to treat, resolve and judge questions of honour on principles of private justice, foreign to the law; in the inclination—especially marked where, as in Sicily, the sense of *amour propre* is very high—to regard every attack on one's person or one's goods as an insult rather than an injury; in the hatred of informers and the reluctance to denounce crime—especially where political considerations enter. In this last connection people are apt to forget that while an informer is vile, the denunciation of crime is the action of an honest man.

In the lower strata of society, however, as time went on, the original idea of *omertà* inevitably degenerated. It still existed, but, with the progressive improvement of political systems and ideas, it was no longer the attribute of rebels against the oppressive and tyrannous governments, but that of exiles from the common law and moral order. It was perverted in its fundamental essence.

Its original dignity turned into boastfulness, its bravery into insolence, its practical judgment into cynical indifference, its self-control into deceit and concealment; from reaction against oppression it turned to aggression, from self-justice to common crime, from the silence of good men through solidarity to the silence of bad men from complicity, and from resistance to oppressive governments to rebellion against moral order and state justice.

Thus it was that *omertà*, by its degradation in the lower circles of society, became and remained a specific attribute of the criminal classes, asserting itself in a formula which is the common creed of crime in all countries and is the present and current meaning of the word *omertà:*

1. Refusal to recognise the legal power;

2. Direct action (getting one's rights by one's own hand);

3. Silence.

This formula, of three interdependent terms, is the law of the criminal classes: implying a particular conception of honour and enforced by very severe sanctions. In Sicily the criminal who violates it is called *'nfatne* (infamous), and is punished by his comrades with ostracism, contempt, mutilation, or death, according to circumstances.

The predominant characteristic even of degenerate *omertà* is rigid and absolute silence. It is the cold, hard, often stoical, silence, which in time past brave men kept under torture. Question by torture, indeed, apart from all its other evil consequences, endowed the silence of criminals with a tinge of heroism and gave rise to the now obsolete custom of educating young criminals to silence by accustoming them to bear pain without flinching. In course of time this gave criminals a certain facility in pretending to have suffered maltreatment, either to support a boast of silence or as an excuse for having spoken before justice.

In this connection a significant occurrence is quoted by the King's Procurator-General Sampietro in an account of his judicial labours:

"In the matter of this maltreatment, which is now a common reason given to explain the retractation of confessions or of admissions of complicity, I may say that in the prison of Castrogiovanni the prisoner, Rizzo Gaetano, accused of belonging to a criminal association, was found to have sewn up in the belt of his breeches a letter to his wife in which he wrote that in her appearance before the chief magistrate that was to take place she must deny her words and say: 'the police-sergeant and others forced me to say this by beating.'"

The law of silence, as it relates to criminals, aims especially at removing all that pertains to the development of criminal activities from the knowledge, control and action of State justice and from the sanction of the law.

The criminal, therefore, does not report his losses or injuries to the police. He keeps silence and reserves reprisals, vengeance and the repair of his losses to himself. Equally, the criminal who is responsible for, or somehow involved in, or merely cognizant of, a crime, keeps silence, refuses to confess and strenuously denies everything, on his own account and on that of his accomplices, accessories and witnesses. It is a form of silence that goes from mutism to absolute denial, but which may, according to circumstances, take on the cloak of reticence, of false witness or of favourable testimony. It may even go further, in fact, as far as calumny. This happens when the criminal, in order to divert justice from himself or his companions or to inculpate somebody else—especially if such a one is guilty of violating the laws of *omertà*—gives false evidence against a third person. But silence may go further still, even to stoicism, to calumny against himself. This is typical of the iron discipline existing in those classes, and thus it often happens that, either spontaneously or by the decision of his comrades, a criminal confesses himself the author of a crime he has not committed, or at least admits his guilt before justice, for the purpose of saving somebody whom it is the common interest to save or simply to redeem himself from some serious offence of *lèse-omertà*.

# The Mafia, And Its Logic

In Scicily the movement of which I have just spoken led not only to the *omertà* that specifically belongs to criminal life, but brought about a special local phenomenon—the Mafia. It was unavoidable. As I have explained, in Sicily, from reasons that have to do with the special character of the island's history, the primal *omertà* was not only more pronounced, but had also developed its own particular tendency to interpose between the constituted power (so far as it was arbitrary and oppressive) and the subject people, and to take overt action with the aim of redressing wrongs or defending individuals and the community. It was natural and inevitable that this tendency, reflected in the lower *strata* of society, should be corrupted and perverted by the same evil influences that had completely swept away the original characteristics of *omertà*. That, indeed, is what happened: and there followed a complex degeneration which, as is easily intelligible, took somewhat ambiguous forms in the course of its development—forms which particularly attracted the attention of observers and students of the period and profoundly touched the heart of the people.

I allude to the so-called chivalrous banditry which, legend apart, has left concrete, though few and sporadic, traces, and on which I touch for a moment simply to point out that it was an episodic and *intermediate* phenomenon, characteristic of the time of transition in the degenerative process. This process, in the course of time, ended in a special form of oppressive tyranny, tinged with boasting and veiled in deceit; it fixed itself parasitically on the country and gathered to itself all the criminals of the island, constraining them to adopt a point of view calculated, above all, to monopolise and exploit all criminal initiative and activity, to remove crime from penal sanctions and to invest itself with the function of negotiating between criminals and populace, gearing the machinery of both to itself in complete defiance of all law and therefore of the State. That was the Mafia.

A specific characteristic of the Mafia, among others, and a particularly interesting one for us here, was that of substituting itself for the State power in all relations between the criminal forces and the people. The result was that, whereas there are everywhere three terms in the struggle to defend society from crime, namely, State, people and criminal classes, in Sicily there were four terms, State, people, Mafia and criminal classes. And that has not always been kept in mind.

I do not know the origin of the word "Mafia," and I do not think I am alone in that. But I have said above what, in my opinion, it represents. I do not deny, and it cannot be denied, that in far-off days and at certain times the word "Mafia" may have had various meanings. There are some, for example, who hold that in it something merely complimentary is implied, so that to call a person or a thing *mafiuso*, as the people pronounce the word, would amount to calling it fine, lively or conspicuous. It is true that the word *mafiuso* is sometimes used in that sense, but it is only a jocular form derived from the outward characteristics of the true *mafiusi* who, especially in country districts, have indeed a tendency to conspicuous appearance.

On the other hand, there are many who see in the Mafia a kind of historic residuum, with an underlying sentimental and chivalrous quality. In my opinion this is an error which comes from the confusion of the genuine figure of the *man,* as it arose in Sicily by direct reflection of the primal *omertà* on the island character (which certainly has an underlying sentimental and chivalrous quality) with the figure of the *mafioso,* who is a degeneration of the man. Indeed, to say of a person in Sicily today that he is a *man* has an honourable meaning, but to say that he is *mafioso* has a very different meaning. At all events, it is certain that a chivalrous Mafia does not exist, unless by chivalrous Mafia you mean a Mafia on horseback. That I *have* seen; but I have also seen it in carriages, in motors, in sleeping-cars and elsewhere. Besides, the words of the Duce ring too sharply here for me to insist on this point: "Gentlemen, it is time that I showed the Mafia up to you. But first of all I want to divest this association of brigands of any kind of fascination or poetry, to which it has not the least claim. Let nobody speak of the nobility or chivalry of the Mafia, unless he really wishes to insult the whole of Sicily."[5]

Finally, there are those who hold that the Mafia is not a criminal force and those who, on the contrary, confuse the Mafia with criminality. For my part, I believe, that the Mafia is a distinct and separate thing from the criminal classes, but only in so far as it is supercriminal. I mean that in the army of crime, criminals represent the rank and file, while the Mafia is the general staff, or that while the criminals at large constitute the muscular system, the Mafia is the brain. Mafia and criminals, however, are akin in spirit and united in a unique creed of which the Mafia furnishes the priests and the criminals are the faithful.

Many people think that the Mafia, by its very nature, is an all-embracing phenomenon. That is not so. On the contrary, there are large zones and entire provinces of Sicily—especially on the eastern side—which have either been immune from the Mafia or have always shown themselves antagonistic to it. And there are many other districts in which the Mafia was a foreign element, imported or imposed. The home centres of the Mafia are few— certainly fewer than is generally supposed. They are necessarily to be found in places where, owing to topographical conditions or to traditional states of mind, the conception and action of the State has most slowly penetrated; and they have been formed for particular, local reasons which have either vanished with time or become confused legends. It is a fact, whether through the reflected influence of the ancient eastern civilisation or of the waves of barbaric invasion and of the foreign dominations that

5    From the speech of Mussolini to the Chamber of Deputies on May 26th, 1927.

ensued, the Mafia declines in intensity as you go from west to east, from the interior to the sea, from the hills to the plains, even to the extent of disappearing entirely.

The Mafia, being essentially parasitic, is not, and cannot be, found among the workers, if by "workers" is meant those in every class who have the will and capacity to make work their means of livelihood or their spring of life and their badge of citizenship. Nor does it, nor can it, exist among the humble, the weak and the dispossessed. Distress may give rise to crime, but could not produce the Mafia. The Mafia lives on the rich, the strong and the powerful, but this does not bring it to the side of the poor or the derelict. In fact, in the play of social oppositions, it is directly opposed to them; in the first place, because with them the Mafia has everything to lose and nothing to gain, and in the second because poverty often means honesty, with which the Mafia does not go hand in hand.

Many people suppose that the Mafia is an association, in the sense of being a vast aggregate organised and incorporated on regular principles, although the outward forms are more or less masked or hidden. I have often been asked what signs of recognition among themselves the *mafiosi* have, what is their hierarchy, what the rules of admission, what the system of appointing chiefs, what the secret laws, the methods of administration and of dividing the profits, and so on: but in reality nothing of this kind exists. It has happened at certain times and in certain districts that the *mafiosi* habitually met in groups which had all the characteristics of true association, with regular and, of course, secret statutes, concealed badges and marks of recognition, definite hierarchies and elections of chiefs; but these were exceptional cases, or cases of a special and sporadic nature. The Mafia, as I am describing it, is a peculiar way of looking at things and of acting which, through mental and spiritual affinities, brings together in definite, unhealthy attitudes men of a particular temperament, isolating them from their surroundings into a kind of caste. It is a potential state which normally takes concrete form in a system of local oligarchies closely interwoven, but each autonomous in its own district. There are no marks of recognition; they are unnecessary. The *mafiosi* know one another partly by their jargon, but mostly by instinct. There are no statutes. The law of *omertà* and tradition are enough. There is no election of chiefs, for the chiefs arise of their own accord and impose themselves. There are no rules of admission. When a candidate has all the necessary qualifications, he is absorbed automatically: and he is automatically expelled, or, if need be, done away with, if he loses them. The rule for the division of the profits is the right of the strongest and *pipa* (silence). That is all.

However, I do not mean that the Mafia is not an association. It is one from a particular point of view, from the view of the penal law, that is. This it is essentially and on its own despite, independently of its actions, and of all the forms of association that it may notoriously use in the development of its criminal activities against persons and property. Whatever form it takes and in whatever way it acts the Mafia, simply because it is what it is, assumes, in the view of the criminal law, the typical shape of an association for criminal purposes against the administration of justice.

*The Mafioso.* It follows from what I have said of the Mafia that the *mafioso* is in a permanent state of criminal responsibility, and is therefore liable to proceedings and to punishment at the hands of the law. But it is not easy to catch him. The difficulty lies not so much in proving that the *mafioso*, simply as such, is involved in a criminal association, but—and it is a more serious difficulty than is supposed—in proving that an individual is in fact a member of the Mafia. This is very difficult to prove, and also proof can only be admitted after the most careful scrutiny, since the appellation of *mafioso* is bandied about with complete recklessness, from ignorance or carelessness, and often in complete bad faith. This occurs in every walk of life, including the political, as a means of accomplishing vendettas, working off old scores, overcoming opponents, damaging competitors, interfering with activities, and so on. And the *mafioso* has, in his turn, acquired a special facility for disguising himself as a persecuted politician, a victim of other people's rancour, or a misunderstood martyr.

The inquiry, therefore, is a matter of some delicacy, especially since, unlike the activities of the ordinary criminal, ex-prisoner or recidivist, which take specific, unmistakable and provable forms, the activities of the *mafioso*, as we shall see, take on a rather ambiguous, doubtful and indefinable aspect. Even the sight of his penal certificate is curious. The ordinary ex-prisoner, of course, presents a penal certificate in which convictions largely prevail: the *mafioso*, on the contrary, is not necessarily "prejudiced" in the eye of the law. He may very well be so, but often he is not. And when he is, he presents a penal certificate in which discharges or releases for want of evidence prevail. These are, usually, the result of compulsory local *omertà*, and the *mafioso* is particularly proud of them, either because, poor fellow, he does not like being convicted, or because in these discharges he mainly sees a victory over State justice redounding to his own greater prestige. But he will avail himself of them, if the opportunity arises, to prove himself a victim of injustice, calumny or judicial error. So, as you see, it is not so easy to define a *mafioso* as to describe the Mafia.

One can only tell a *mafioso* by intuition: one guesses, or smells him. And it can only be brought home to him by intent observation and by catching him in definite acts which, having escaped the man's own watchful self-control, reveal and prove his unmistakable psychological trend. The *mafioso* is an involved and complex figure. He is a bully, but an actor and a humbug. So that one sometimes supposes a man is a *mafioso*, and he turns out only to be a fool; and *vice versa*. As a result, the measures of prevention are diffident, whence it happens that, in the desire not to be too lenient, mistakes are very often made in being too severe. These mistakes are sometimes glaring and profoundly unjust. I have often heard, for instance, honest men called *mafiosi* in perfect good faith only because, being particularly resolute, courageous and resentful of oppression, they reacted in direct, violent and extra-legal ways against a malefactor, without resorting to the authorities. These are honest men, rough and primitive generally, in whom the primal and pure *omertà* has expressed itself with particular vigour in the manly intent to assert justice, right and human dignity against the uncurbed ascendancy of crime.

Thus, there is an authentic anti-Mafia, in which some have seen a form of Mafia, antagonistic indeed to other forms, but akin to them in its common tendency to illegality, to violence and to disregard of legal power. But those who think so forget that the Mafia is a degenerate thing and a preordained breaking of legal precepts, while pure *omertà* is an essentially sane, but sometimes excessive force, and that, while it may sometimes go against the law, it only does so far in committing an actual offence and in somewhat too widely interpreting the right of legitimate self-defence. I will take an instance from a report by the late Signor Liguori, an excellent magistrate and at the time King's Procurator at Trapani—who, after comparing the country folks' listlessness in helping the police with their energy in trying to get their own back, said:—

"A curious and interesting example of the fierce antagonism between plunderers and plundered is to be found in a fight that took place one night at M. Some cattle-raiders had raided some cattle there, having bound and maltreated the little herdboy who, as soon as he saw them depart, informed his employers, the P——. The P—— set out in pursuit and came in view of the robber caravan; they opened fire, and a lively battle ensued, with heavy rifle-fire—a complete strategic action fought over a wide stretch of country in the heart of the night, as each side skirmished and groped and laid ingenious ambushes for the other. After a night-long battle the malefactors succeeded in taking refuge in the impenetrable forest of S. But the P-turned them out of this too, and successfully launched the final attack. At dawn they recaptured the abandoned booty and retired. As usual, the names of the defeated robbers are not known; and it is supposed that the man S-who has disappeared, lost his life on that night of bloodshed."

So much for what Signor Liguori says. On my own part, I may add that the P-got into a good deal of trouble afterwards and were called *mafiosi* for having *taken justice into their own hands!*

Another very common tendency is to give the appellation of *mafiosi* to the owners of the great landed estates of the island, on account of the distinct preference that they are supposed to have for letting the land, or for handing over the management of agricultural holdings, to members of the Mafia. But here too there is often injustice. The great landed estates of Sicily, long left defenceless through the indifference of the State and particularly exposed to attack by malefactors, had to provide for their own protection; and they were compelled, under threat of ruin, to come to terms with the Mafia, either by letting the land to them on extorted terms (whence arose the hated figure of the Mafia in the shape of the *gabellotto* [6], which did so much harm to agriculture in the island), or by accepting and paying the men whom the Mafia designated to guarantee the safety of their undertakings. Hence the unfortunately notorious company of *campieri, soprastanti, guardiani* and the like (guardians of *latifondi* [7] and holdings) who, being members of the Mafia and being named by it, while in fact they kept landed property subject to the Mafia, assumed the garb of its custodians and gave the ignorant the outward appearance of being so. In reality, therefore, the *gabellotti, campieri, soprastanti* and the like, being a typical expression of a dominant rural Mafia, were not, as many still think, direct and spontaneous products of the large estates, but were their chief parasites. They were the agents and the proof of the *régime* of compulsion to which the landowners were subjected by the Mafia itself and against which they rose at once no sooner did the State—and it was the Fascist State—give concrete signs of its presence and its will. Another mistake, the most serious and unjust, is to attribute the quality of *mafioso* by right of inheritance.

---

6  Tenant

7  Vast estates of rather poor ground, like the Scotch forests.

The young, even today, are particularly liable to have this appellation conferred on them. It is not, as a rule, very definite; but even so, it is often more than enough to spoil a man's career. "He would be a nice young fellow," people say in such cases, "and is full of promise, only his father (or his grandfather or great-grandfather or uncle or more or less distant relation) is (or was even thirty years ago) a *mafioso*" That is enough. Through that diffidence in prevention of which I have already spoken, the nice young fellow often becomes, in the eyes of anybody who has heard those words, a sort of candidate for the Mafia, or simply a hereditary *mafioso*. And it is easy to imagine the consequences. Among others there is this: that, whereas the Mafia by passage of time and evolution of consciousness under the restoring breeze of Fascism is rapidly declining, its shadow is perpetuated in this way, and an artificial, false and deplorable continuity is created between the past and the present. I do not deny for a moment that unhealthy tendencies may be inherited, but one ought not to exaggerate their influence to the extent of complete loss of confidence. If such young fellows were guided confidently on to the right way of life and given liberty of movement and room to breathe, you would see, far oftener than is supposed, sons and grandsons of *mafiosi* no longer slipping back into the old bad ways, but marching onwards to redeem in their own lives the possible faults of their sires and grandsires—or some of them.

*The Logic of the Mafia.* As I have said before, the Mafia has no statutes, but derives its rules and discipline from *omertà*, understood as the law of the criminal classes. And it gets a particular power from a special form of logic which is worth while getting to know, though it is neither mysterious nor abstruse. Consistently with its mentality, the Mafia neither perceives nor recognises the ethical content of the social struggle against crime: it sees it simply as a question of material damage. Starting from the almost mystical conception that crime exists and must exist since it was created, not only does it deny all effectiveness to the legal provisions for combating it, but considers the struggle against crime, as understood and practised by the instruments of social defence, an error, a useless waste of energy, and an act against nature, whether it be repressive or preventive. Of the latter form of defence, especially when tending to the removal of temptation to crime through better education, it not only asserts that it is useless, but that, as a weapon, it is dangerous.

"You talk a lot about the fight against illiteracy," a man of the Mafia said to me once. "Fight away, then. But this is what will happen. The boy who today, being illiterate, can only deliver other people's swindling letters, will no sooner have learned to read and write than he will write them for himself and get other illiterates to deliver them."

When the Mafia expresses its outlook in that kind of concrete way, not only is it being coherent with the ethical inversion that characterises its psychology, but it is obeying an instinct of self-defence which induces it to attack what it feels to be its principal enemy, namely, education, by depreciating its value—having no other weapon. The Mafia, instinctively and obscurely, but without doubt, fears the prison less than the school, where its own conservation is concerned; especially the poor, isolated school, which means an outpost of education among the humble and the far-away. It fears the judge less than the schoolmaster, especially the schoolmaster who can sway the boys' minds by manly suggestion or by persuasive gentleness. It fears the *carabiniere* less than the boys of the *Balilla*, especially the tiniest, those nearest the cradle and so most amenable to influence. And it fears the musket less than the plough.

This is natural and perfectly logical. The *carabiniere*, the judge and the prison may make gaps in the ranks of the Mafia, but these gaps, being more or less temporary, can be filled up almost at once by the continuous influx of new recruits; and so the army remains, perpetually at war, but perpetually efficient. But the school, the schoolmaster and the *Balilla* strike at the root of the Mafia. They obstruct it by diverting the influx of new forces; they directly spoil its recruitment; and they mathematically lead to its exhaustion through lack of new blood, in a more or less short period of time, while the plough not only takes living and active men away from it, but hands them over to the enemy.

At this point, however, it is my duty to declare that, in spite of all, the Mafia admits, nay, accepts with noisy enthusiasm, another notion—the notion of *redemption*. And it practises it with a peculiar fervour. Naturally in its own way, but, failing anything better, even this is something. I had definite proof of this one day when, having declared to some hundred peasants that the fight against crime was to be conducted on the plain principle of "making a fresh start, that is, redeeming yourself in the way of honest work, or disappearing," the first to break into shouts of approval were some well-known figures of the Mafia (some twenty champions) who up till that moment had been clinging to the outskirts of the crowd, like prickly brambles round a flowery meadow. They were redeemed men, or men to be redeemed by acquired right. There was nothing strange in this.

When an active and intelligent *mafioso*, by proceedings which it would be useless to go into, once you admit that the end justifies the means, succeeds—and he always succeeds—in getting a little bit of property together; when, for example, by threats, shooting and other such humorous methods, he has succeeded in getting leased to himself, at 20 per cent of its true value, a fat piece of land, which the pious ox (regularly recruited by similar means) placidly renders fertile; then, at the sight of this Virgilian spectacle of tranquil labour and prosperous peace, the *mafioso* grows soft-hearted, feels himself seized with love for the human race and—redeems himself. Quite simple, since stamped paper, certificates and the like are not necessary. He redeems himself by himself, automatically. That is to say, he pardons himself for his own misdeeds and goes over, arms and baggage (including, of course, land, oxen and the rest) to rest in the shadow of his country's laws and enjoy in peace the fruits of his hard work.

He becomes a man of order—rigidly, almost fiercely, a man of order. And he holds out as long as he can. That is, until some old comrade, who has remained a proletarian, squares things up with a musket-shot; or until, by the necessity of events or by the overwhelming revival of his instincts (for the leopard cannot change his spots) he sees an opportunity to unredeem himself temporarily, only to redeem himself again when the business is over. Whence one sees the moving sight of the multi-redeemed and the super-redeemed man: a kind of Saint Antony who, if he is not able, like the real one, to resist temptation, at least knows how to profit by it. Usually there is formed round these redeemed men a more or less obligatory atmosphere of tacit acquiescence. Let sleeping dogs lie. And so the redemption wears itself out.

After which, what I have called the logic of the Mafia hastens to its conclusion, which is this. Since crime exists, since it is a vain dream to think of destroying it, and since it has a vitality of its own which it is waste of time to think of repressing or preventing, there is only one practical way of dealing with it. And that is to recognise it and to dominate it sufficiently to discipline its activities, to control its initiative and to balance the losses by levelling up, that is by adjustment between the little tributary pressure that it represents and the contributive capacity of the locality in general and of the individual inhabitants in particular. One should intervene then, as against crime, but only with the aim of reducing the damage done: therefore, the crime itself is to be removed from the cognizance of the authorities, who are foolish enough to think otherwise, and negotiations are to be set on foot between the malefactors and the injured. This is not simply a deduction of my own: it is a definite and clear assertion which, often in very picturesque forms, I have more than once heard, and it is summed up in a characteristic phrase of the Mafia: "*Li picciuotti hanno a vivere!*" (The brigands have a right to live too!)

But that is not all. Owing to the serious and persistent failure of State action against the spread of crime, additional arguments reinforced these claims (I speak of now remote times). "It is useless arguing," people said: "the facts show that, in spite of all the instruments, means, laws, codes and proceedings of which they dispose, and in spite of the science on which they draw, the authorities know only a very small part of the criminal classes. They succeed with difficulty, when they do succeed, in identifying the author of a crime, they have great difficulty in repairing the damage, and they feel themselves, on the whole, so little masters of the truth, that they have adopted as conclusive the middle term of the so-called *guilt non-proven* or *insufficient evidence*. The Mafia is quite different. With its system, without need of a whole herd of officials, it has complete knowledge of the criminal classes in its neighbourhood, their springs of action, their tendencies and their individual elements. It always knows all the authors of every crime and feels itself in every case so much a master of the truth that it admits no middle terms. When it liquidates anybody, no anxiety lest it has made a mistake disturbs it. It knows perfectly what it is doing." And people said more than this. They said: "When a crime has been committed, the authorities are mainly concerned to find its author; the Mafia bothers about nothing but the damage done, and this, in the great majority of cases, is what most interests those who have suffered. In this field the Mafia obtains far greater successes than the authorities.

Suppose, for example, that cattle to the value of 100,000 lire have been stolen. *First case.* The person robbed has recourse to the authorities, and they take decided action. Going by the official statistics of cattle-raiding, in seventy-five per cent of cases (these arguments refer to many years ago) the authorities find out nothing; in fifteen per cent of the cases they find out the actual authors of the crime (mere tools with no means from whom there is nothing to be recovered) but do not recover the lost property; and in only ten per cent of the cases, whether they do or do not discover the authors, do they succeed in recovering the stolen cattle. For the man who has been robbed, therefore, there are ten chances of complete recovery of his property against ninety chances of entire loss, *plus* expenses of travelling to hearings, confrontations, recognitions, evidence, etc., *plus* loss of time; *plus* the probability of reprisals.

"*Second case*. The injured person goes to the Mafia. The Mafia compiles no statistics, but admits that in five per cent of the cases it fails. There is an underworld of crime which escapes its control and sometimes there are reasons why it cannot act as it would like. But in ninety-five per cent of the cases the Mafia (in connivance with the authors of the crime with whom it settles matters) recovers the lost property which it gives back to the robbed person in return for payment of about a third of its value. So that, in the instance in question, the stolen cattle worth 100,000 lire would be restored by the Mafia on payment of 30,000 lire, including everything, even its own kind intervention. The robbed person, therefore, has five chances of losing his cattle completely against 95 chances of getting them back on terms involving a loss of 30 per cent.

To sum up and compare the two possibilities: as against the ten chances of entire restitution that the authorities can offer the robbed person, the Mafia offers him ninety-five chances of restitution at a loss of 30 per cent; and as against the ninety chances of total loss of the stolen cattle which the authorities offer him, the Mafia only offers five, and that without travelling expenses, without loss of time and without the probability of reprisals. Indeed, the Mafia offers also a kind of insurance against future robbery, since in this kind of transactions there is an implicit undertaking by the Mafia to obviate the possibility of repetitions. And there is this special difference too: that while the authorities ask the robbed person to speak out (which is not always healthy), the Mafia simply asks him to hold his tongue (which is undoubtedly more comfortable and useful); and while the authorities, what with inquiries, examinations, trials and the like take some years to come to a conclusion, the Mafia, without any talk or fuss, finishes the matter in a few days—a very important consideration."

That is what people thought and said. I need not spend any longer on the point, since the example I have given is enough to show what the logic of the Mafia is capable of, what a power of perfidious suggestion it can exercise and what harm it can do in surroundings where the defence against crime has become relegated to individuals and is treated by them as a private matter outside the law, owing to the permanent deficiency of legal protection and the persistence of losses. Thus it was that the Mafia was able to make the whole machinery work to its own advantage, not only by subjugating the perpetrators of crime, absorbing their powers of initiative and monopolising their most profitable activities in its own interest, while placing the people under direct contribution; but also by exploiting both, people and malefactors, a second time by assuming the garb of intermediary in negotiations between the two parties. The mediation, of course, was not given for nothing to either party, but yet it was so far effective that it has often been said that the Mafia was a factor in moderating crime!

That was how it became possible for the Mafia to substitute itself for the law in the relations between criminals and their victims and to divert the fight against crime in the direction of compromise, completely outside the purview of the social power, which, being automatically excluded, thus found itself confronted with a very serious obstacle, silence. This silence was implicit in the very fact of the compromise, it being understood that, from the moment the injured parties entered into negotiation with the malefactors through the good offices of the Mafia, they assumed the obligation of absolute silence towards the authorities. And this silence, although compulsory or, in some cases, due to a sort of honourable feeling, spread abroad like a subtle infection through suggestion, through prejudice, through fear of reprisals, through hopeless mistrust of the legal power and, above all, through the necessity to live; and it created, by compulsion, a sort of local solidarity which tended to elude the repressive action of the law. Hence the numerous obligatory ways in which even the victims of crime either refused to give evidence or gave false evidence in the interest of those who had robbed them or otherwise injured them. It was clear that they did so under protest, but that could not be proved. On the contrary, it was said that they acted in the spirit of *omertà* ingrained in Sicilians through their instinctive tendency to general complicity in crime.

And that was the bitter irony of it.

# Typical Traits Of The Mafia

I could illustrate what I have said in the last chapter by numerous examples, but I will limit myself to a few typical cases which date a good many years back. Here is one. A peasant once had his mule stolen. Scruples of conscience made him report the theft to the authorities, but at the same time he applied to the Mafia and set negotiations on foot for the recovery of his animal. It so happened that, two days later, the authorities sequestrated in another village, and in the hands of the very intermediary to whom the peasant had applied for the recovery of his mule, a number of mules which had evidently been stolen. When, as is usual in such cases, all those in the district who had suffered robbery were summoned—and among them our friend—to see if any of their animals was in the group that had been seized, the man, taking a rapid glance at the animals, definitely declared that his mule was not there. It was an obvious lie: and the mule herself proved it, for she was in the group and, at the sound of her master's voice as he denied her presence, she broke into such manifestations of affection that there was no possible doubt as to her identity. And the man himself was not unaffected, since, in spite of his impassable features, the coolness of his attitude and the obstinacy of his denial, two silent little tears, bearing witness to his feelings, gathered in the corners of his eyes. All the same, he persisted in non-recognition.

Recourse was then had to another of the customary methods of proof. The mule was brought by night to the peasant's village, and was set free where the houses began. She made quietly for the door of her owner's house and was welcomed there with cries of joy by his wife, his children and the neighbours. "Well," the peasant was asked—for he had arrived and witnessed the scene— "is this your house? Is this your family? Are these your neighbours?"

"Yes," he answered.

"So the mule is yours."

"I did not say so."

"But the others say so."

"Anyhow, we will leave the mule in your charge provisionally, and then we'll see."

"As the *Signora Giustizia* wishes."

And the good man, at peace with his conscience, embraced his mule, calling by the tenderest names.

"After all," he probably said to himself, "I didn't say the mule was mine: it was the mule who said I was her master."

Another case. One day, when cattle-raiding was very bad, about five hundred sheep suspected of being stolen were seized in the hands of certain malefactors. The people of the district who had been robbed having been brought together to recognise their own animals, an old shepherd (who had been robbed of a hundred head some months before) chose some thirty sheep from the whole number and declared that they were his and that they belonged to the group stolen from him. It having sometimes happened that not over-scrupulous men sometimes falsely recognised animals that were not theirs in such cases, the shepherd was removed, and the thirty sheep, after a hidden mark had been made with shears in the wool under their bellies, were dispersed in the herd again. The shepherd was then brought in again and asked to identify his animals. Without hesitation he picked the thirty sheep out one by one. There was no doubt, therefore, as to his recognition of them. And the sheep, branded on the cheek with a special police mark, were handed over to their owner who drove them away.

Regular judicial proceedings were, of course, opened against the men who had been arrested with the animals in their possession. It was then that the Mafia intervened. It got into touch with the shepherd and induced him to retract in court his previous recognition of the animals, assuring him that he would suffer no loss since the value of the animals would be paid to him. So it was that, at the hearing of the case, our man completely withdrew his recognition. Neither arguments nor proofs to the contrary were any use. "I made a mistake," he said. *"Bedda Matri!* (Holy Mother!) I thought they were mine, but I can't honestly swear to them." And nothing else could be got out of him. The inevitable result was the acquittal of the thieves and the restoration to them of the thirty sheep.

But when our man went back to his "friends" to ask for the price of his sheep according to the agreement, he was told to hold his tongue and to thank God that, after the *infamità* he had committed in recognising his sheep the first time, he had got off with a whole skin. "That's all very well," the man replied. *"Infamità* be blowed, but a contract is a contract, and you must pay me." And he went off so set on legally summoning the Mafia for not fulfilling the famous contract that, when somebody pointed out the absurdity of the position, he grumbled with a shake of his curly black head: "Is there no law, then?" And so, while holding to his retraction of recognition, he applied for a summons; but of course there could only be one ending to the matter.

Things did not always end like this, however. On another occasion during the same period a shepherd unequivocally recognised as his and as belonging to a flock which had been stolen from him a few months before fifty sheep and a ram which were included in a large number of sheep seized in the hands of the relations of two *latitanti:* he took over the animals and began his long journey home. By order of the authorities, who had observed—as usually happens in cases where a large number of animals has been seized—some suspicious-looking figures moving about, two armed policemen escorted him. After walking for two hours, however, the shepherd who perhaps was ashamed to be seen with an escort as he neared his own village, told the policemen that now he felt perfectly safe and that they could go home with easy minds. The road was straight and flat, the country bare and deserted as far as the eye could see, and in front, a few kilometers off, his village perched on a hill. The policemen saw no reason to go any further and so, yielding to the shepherd's plea, they turned back. No more than half-an-hour later, as the shepherd was cheerfully going on his way, four masked individuals, armed with muskets, jumped out from under a little bridge where they had been hiding and confronted him. They clearly knew him and he knew them. They said nothing: there was no need. The shepherd, guilty of broken *omertà* through having recognised his sheep in court, knew what to expect. Without a word, while two of them held him fast, the other two took the ram out of the flock and, soaking his fleece in paraffin which they had brought with them, set fire to it. The horrible scene that followed did not last long, and the poor animal fell dead.

"You see what we did to your ram?" the criminals said to the poor shepherd. "Now we're going to do the same to you."

The unhappy man's prayers were of no avail. The four criminals soaked his hair and clothes with paraffin, set him on fire and then let him go, looking on without blenching at the horrible scene which ended with his death. This tragedy would be enough by itself to put in their true light the terms of the old problem of public safety in Sicily: but, in this particular connection, it gives a pretty clear idea of the danger incurred by those who found themselves by chance or by the necessity of things hemmed in between the Mafia and the police. Their situation was often very difficult, and that explains the ambiguity of certain attitudes and people.

I remember a typical case. In a village where the Mafia was particularly well-developed, some years ago, there arose a young *latitante* who soon made his name known for boldness and brutality. Naturally, the police gave chase; a certain police-sergeant was particularly active. One day, having come down unobserved from the hills to the village, the *latitante* went in search of that sergeant and, having found him while he was leading his little son by the hand, shot him with his pistol, wounding him in the abdomen, luckily not seriously. The sergeant, although wounded, bravely tried to pursue him, but failed to catch him. In view of the seriousness of the occurrence I decided to go to the place myself: and since I knew that the *latitante* in question had a special place of refuge on the land of a certain person, I reached the village after dark, entered it alone and unobserved, and went to this man's house. I entered and found my way to a small room where my friend was sitting in solitary digestive meditation.

At my first appearance, seeing me dressed in the local fashion with a *scapolare* (hooded overcoat) on my back, he did not recognise me but was visibly disturbed. When I revealed who I was, he was still more perturbed. My words were brief and to the point: "I know that, for love or by compulsion, you harbour the *latitante* X," I said. "Now tell me at once where I can find him to-night. I am alone, nobody knows me, nobody saw me come in and I shall disappear as I came; so you can be quite easy on your own account. But, either you tell me where he is, and quickly, or. . . ."

Dead silence on the man's part; drops of sweat at the roots of his hair; looks that almost invoked the witness of Heaven against my unseasonable intrusion; and other sad looks at a box where probably there was something stronger than sweets. Finally he gurgled "B-but. . . ." A few accessory arguments on my part, reinforced by a few expressive exclamations; half-words, heavy with obscure threats. Protestations of innocence on the other side, anxious reflection and then, at last, "Your hand!" my friend said. A meaning clasp of the hand, a sigh, and then: "I am not sure, but I think the *latitante* is tonight at-." Here he described the place, which was a kind of hut among large rocks, looking on to an impenetrable path halfway up the neighbouring mountain, about an hour and a half's walk from the village. All right! I went away unobserved as I had come, followed by sighs and also, without doubt, by my friend's invocation of his departed ancestors for my—good health.

When I got out of the village, I left the horses with two of my men, and with four others, after a very hasty meal on the spot, I went on foot in the direction indicated. It really was an impenetrable path, and this made us lose a good deal of time. We reached the neighbourhood of the hut at a late hour of the night. It had one door and two windows, and no other apparent exit. There was no dog, no noise. Complete darkness and silence. The rocks rose up a few yards away, making a circle of granite round the hut. There was nothing to be done but wait for dawn. So, posting my men behind the rocks that commanded the door and windows, I waited. The sky was slowly getting light when a noise was heard in the hut. A light was lit, somebody coughed. Look out! Suddenly the door opened and the figure of a man was outlined against the lighted space. After a moment's hesitation he came out into the open. Apparently he had no long weapon, and his face could not be seen as it was hidden by the hood of his *scapolare*, below which, however, appeared a good pair of riding boots heavily spurred. Having taken a long look at the sky and the mountainside, the man turned his back on us and began to go in. It was the moment. Coming out from my rock, I was on him in a bound and, pointing the barrel of my Winchester at his head, I ordered him to halt. The man turned round at once.

"You!" I exclaimed.

"You! And on foot!" exclaimed he.

It was not the *latitante*. It was simply the individual with whom I had spoken the preceding evening. In the serious dilemma in which I had placed him, in the first moment of weakness, he had told me the *latitante's* hiding-place: and then, having thought better of it, and probably fearing that the sound of the horses which I usually went about with might give alarm to the *latitante* himself, who would not have failed to hold him, the only person aware of his hiding-place, to strict account for his treachery, he had mounted his trusty mare and ridden hell for leather by a longer but better way so as to arrive at the hut before me, and in time therefore to warn the bandit of the presence of the police in the neighbourhood. And he had been unable to get away at once, as he would have liked, because the bandit, very suspicious, had ordered him not to move from the hut till daybreak. He confessed all this to me himself and in such a way that I could not be angry with him.

But the thing did not end here, for, having firmly made up my mind to lay hands on the *latitante*, I went back to the village and, having called together some of the locals who were affiliated to the Mafia, I told them that if the bandit had not given himself up within three days or if, at any rate, I had not received the indication of his hiding-place, I would set a train of action on foot that they themselves would remember for many a long day. Naturally they all protested their ignorance and innocence. But when, reminding them that the police-sergeant had been leading his own little child by the hand when the *latitante* tried to murder him, I said that I considered those who would protect the doer of such a deed no less vile and unworthy of pity than the criminal himself, they were stricken with silent embarrassment.

Three days later I got an anonymous letter by post to this effect: "If you want to find the *latitante* - go to the— mountain in the neighbourhood of ..... Precise indications for recognising the spot were given. The general appearance of the letter was not very convincing, but, to make quite sure, I sent some men to the mountain indicated. The *latitante* was certainly there, but dead. He had clearly been killed elsewhere with a couple of bullets in the head and then been brought to that place. An action of the Mafia, without doubt: but nobody could ever find out where, when, and by whose hand, the murder took place.

Those who wonder at the swift certainty of the Mafia's action in this case may like to hear another small but significant episode. Some years ago, in a populous town of the island, a foreigner on his travels had the disagreeable surprise one day of failing to find his wallet in his pocket. Convinced that he had been robbed, he went and told the occurrence to an acquaintance of his in the place, and his friend, instead of going to the authorities, thought it was quicker to go and wait on a certain big gun of the local Mafia. He pointed out to him that, quite apart from the theft in itself, the occurrence was particularly inconvenient as having happened to a foreigner. The big gun found the observation just, said he would look into it, and the following day presented himself with five wallets.

"See if yours is here," he said to the foreigner.

"It is not," he replied.

"What do you mean? It must be. Take a good look."

"Do you mean to say I can't recognise my own wallet? I repeat, it isn't here."

"Impossible. These are the five wallets that were stolen yesterday. There are no others; there couldn't be."

"And how do you know that no others were stolen?"

A discreet smile.

"That may be: but mine isn't here." "Then, my dear sir," said the big gun, "your wallet was not stolen."

To tell the truth, the foreigner was not much pleased by this conclusion. But he resigned himself to his loss and went on board the ship by which he was leaving. But when, in his cabin, he was delving in his portmanteau for maps and clothes, he saw his wallet fall out, having obviously left it in the pocket of one of his coats. The big gun had been right. He knew what he was talking about.

# Crime In Sicily

Now we come to the third term of the series, namely, crime. Crime is innate in human nature and in social life; it is not a transitory phenomenon. Immunity from crime presupposes a state of human and social perfection that has been denied to mankind. Violence and fraud are the common denominators of all forms of crime in all countries.

In Sicily, one of the most singular characteristics of crime is its primitiveness. The Sicilian criminal class, though bold and intelligent, has remained primitive owing to its strong rural element, which is wedded to tradition and antagonistic to progress, and as a natural result of island conditions—a low standard of life, elementary needs, a patriarchal economic system and a highly primitive state of agriculture, industry, commerce and finance. Primitive criminals mean elementary, direct, violent and generally unintelligent action, joint action and the use of arms. Except in cases of banditry, of which I shall speak later, the Sicilian never goes alone or unarmed. Indeed, he has a passion for arms, which often leads to senseless brutality. Once, for instance, five malefactors, armed at all points and masked, took up their position on a country road and assailed the first waggoner who came along, taking from him half a cigar and two coins of twenty *centesimi;* from the next waggoner they took an old leather belt, and because the third waggoner had nothing that could be taken from him, they shot him in the back. Other characteristics of crime in Sicily are the following:

*The absence of the female element,* which is to be explained by the traditional reserve of the Sicilian woman and the strong family sentiment of the island population.

*The abundance of minors,* which is principally due to the physical and physiological precocity of the race and is not more dangerous than their activity in other countries, due to unhealthy intellectual or cerebral precocity.

*The absence of alcoholics, drug-fiends and the like,* the Sicilians being a very abstemious race.

*The abundance of the malarious,* which is due to the preponderance of the rural element and which is undoubtedly a special characteristic, since malarial infection seriously aggravates a tendency to crime by exciting evil passions or encouraging morbid suspicions.

*Excessive quantity,* which some people think is the most striking characteristic of crime in Sicily. But on this point it is unnecessary for me to speak since the truth has been put once and for all by Mussolini, both numerically and in its relation to public safety, when he said: "Five million patriotic Sicilian workers shall no longer be oppressed, put to tribute, robbed and dishonoured by a few hundred criminals."

It is commonly held, and especially since the recent fight against the Mafia confirmed the existence of large criminal associations, that crime in Sicily is a complex organism on associative lines. This is not exactly true. Certainly, as if by contrast to the individualistic tendency of the race, an associative tendency is characteristic of crime in Sicily. This tendency was particularly evident, frequent and serious in crimes against persons and property. But these associative forms are usually casual and always transitory.

The Sicilian criminal is ardent, impulsive and exuberant by nature and he is animated by a strong aggressive spirit; but he is like shifting sand which a gust of wind may condense into temporary heaps of definite shape or whirl about in eddies. There is no essential stability in his combinations.

The official statistics usually reckon the amount of crime by the number of *crimes committed,* which are necessarily identified with the *crimes reported.* But in Sicily this method of calculation won't work. The two figures do not correspond, because not all the crimes committed are denounced, either through a lingering sense of *omertà* or through indifference to the habitual loss or the dangers inseparable from the uncontested domination of crime, or through conviction, born of the State's failure in the fight against crime, that denunciation was no less useless than dangerous. Crimes remain undenounced, too, because fear of injury or reprisal oblige the sufferers, in the lack of any alternative, to settle the matter by negotiation with the criminals, the Mafia, as usual, being the intermediary. And since this kind of fear increases and spreads in proportion to the increase of crime, it follows that the more crimes are committed, the less are reported to the police. In such circumstances the statistics reflect a situation the opposite of the true one. Besides, there were the districts technically immune from crime where, the population being entirely under the thumb of, and tributary to, the Mafia and the criminal classes, crime was unnecessary. In such cases, while in reality the situation embraced one single, permanent, general crime which was the essential sum of innumerable crimes, the figure of crime in the statistics was zero, implying no criminal activity and a perfect state of public safety. There was nothing to be said. In the light of the figures the statistical state was correct, although in the light of the facts these figures were valueless.

The worst feature of crime in Sicily was that it had become completely dominated by the Mafia: the Mafia directed crime and exploited it, to the point that the criminal agencies came to be regarded as substantially a sub-Mafia.

Once, when I was passing through a lonely district in the interior, I chanced to surprise two young armed criminals who were driving a large herd of Maltese goats, obviously stolen, and worth about thirty thousand lire. When told to halt they threatened to use their weapons and serious consequences very nearly ensued.

Under examination they declared—and I found out later they had told the truth—that the day before a certain man, *whom they could not disobey,* had ordered them to go that same night to a ruined and empty barn, take over the herd of goats they would find in it and drive them to another barn some way off and shut them up there—a risky transference of stolen goods. The reward to be given them by the person concerned on their return was to be five lire. Not very much, in comparison with the value of the goats and the danger of the undertaking, while the two poor fellows had not the slightest idea for whose benefit they were risking their liberty and their skin. However, there it was. It might have been worse. It was useless to argue, dangerous to rebel. In the exercise of its prerogatives and disciplinary powers the Mafia was absolute, uncompromising and determined.

A consequence of this was that the Mafia's internal life was a succession of tragic contests, between individuals or between groups. Being formed of a system of local groups which, although bound by a common origin, wanted to be autonomous and alone in their respective districts, it was infected with the germ of frequent intestine struggles for leadership, for supremacy, for the suppression of competition, etc.; and these struggles were rendered particularly fierce by the character of the contestants, by the interests at stake and by the exaggerated sense of *amour propre* that often inspired them. These conflicts gave rise to bloody incidents and reprisals of every kind, and the conciliatory intervention of the "big guns" of the super-Mafia only with difficulty put an end to them. They went on for years and dozens of years, and were handed down from one branch of a family to another till they sometimes ended in the complete annihilation of both parties. Hence the large number of the so-called "Mafia crimes," distinguished by their savagery, their gravity and the impossibility of discovering their authors. The earth was piled with corpses; and to every corpse both populace and authorities hastened to pay what are called their "last respects," heaving a sigh of relief and exclaiming with an air of funereal hopefulness: *"That's one gone!"*; or as often happened: *"Two gone! . . . Three gone! . . .Four gone!"* And so on. On one occasion the number went up to twenty-seven, and then the thing stopped because nothing was left of the contending parties but their boots. And the thing was not without danger to the public. The protagonists in the fight of Mafia against Mafia were all out to win and went straight for victory without caring about anybody or anything. It was dangerous to get in the way.

Once at A-, while one of these desperate and mortal struggles was going on, one of the principals, duly armed with a short double-barrelled gun loaded with shot, had posted himself on the main road with the firm and pious intention of sending to his Creator his enemy, once a much-feared *latitante,* but now in good odour with justice, and about to pass that way. A little later, indeed, the *ex-latitante* appeared. He came without suspicion to within twenty yards of where his enemy was waiting. The latter at once put his gun to his shoulder. Just at that moment two strangers, going about their own business, happened to come into the line of fire. The man in ambush made up his mind in a twinkling. With one shot he dispatched the two unlucky men to get a clear aim, and with the other he found his target and laid his enemy low.

The Mafia, this being the nature of its internal relations, was no less decisive in its relations with criminals in general. From them it demanded complete subordination, absolute obedience and *rispetto* (respect). This last was even required in exterior forms and was understood particularly as a concrete recognition of the prerogative of *immunity* belonging to the *mafioso,* not only in his person but also in everything that he had to do with or that he was pleased to take under his protection. In fine, evildoers had to leave the *mafioso* severely alone, and all the persons or things to which, explicitly or implicitly, he had given a guarantee of security. That is the meaning of the word *rispetto* in this connection.

For instance, among the field-watchmen or *campieri* who had to be taken on and paid by the big landed interests, at the behest of the Mafia, to look after the estates, there was the *campiere di rispetto,* so-called not, as some think, because his employment was an act of respect towards the Mafia, but because he guaranteed the security of the estate of which he was guardian, through the *rispetto* for his person that was due, in a subordinate sense, from the malefactors and, out of solidarity or reciprocity, from the Mafia itself. In fact, the *campiere di rispetto* did not usually carry out the functions of his office continuously or in person, and often he did not even reside on the estate entrusted to his care—or rather which he had seized—but he simply allowed his name to be used. That was usually enough. It is to be noted that the Mafia laid great store by this *rispetto,* not out of concern for personal safety, but for reasons of prestige, since it saw in every injury inflicted upon it by criminals or others an insubordination, an insult or an act of contempt rather than an act of material damage.

In the exercise of its disciplinary powers over the criminal classes the Mafia made no allowance for weakness and allowed no second offence. Its penal sanctions had in view the offences of rebellion, *'nfamità* (violation of the laws of *omertà)* and treachery; and, according to circumstances, persons and events, they took the forms of disqualification and the subsequent abandonment of the offender, *sfregio* (cuts on the face), and death. A victim might sometimes be done away with in so secret a way that, his body having disappeared, doubts as to his fate continued for years; but the murder was often committed in an open and insulting manner. In these cases the corpse of the victim, mutilated in certain symbolic ways, would be left in view of the public with a veil of tragic mystery surrounding it which justice seldom succeeded in penetrating. This was the reason that, from petty roguery to the heights of banditry, crime in Sicily could only gravitate round the Mafia.

But it must not be supposed that this was all secured in a peaceful manner. Crime in Sicily had its irregulars and its outlaws from the constituted order. These were solitary men, disqualified, timid, impatient, novices and the like, who could not adapt themselves to the *régime* of the Mafia or in whom the Mafia had no confidence. In general they were a low class of criminals, accustomed to commit small, though none the less serious, offences, against persons and specially against property. The Mafia often gave them the contemptuous name of *percia-pagliara* (lurkers in straw-stacks), and when they were troublesome it got rid of them with a gun to keep up its prestige.

Sometimes, when they were too numerous and too active, without any *rispetto* for anybody, the Mafia, unable to slaughter them *en masse*, contrived to let them fall into the hands of the police. In this way, while the police carried out a useful operation, the Mafia killed two birds with one stone: that is, it almost seemed to be rendering a service to the police and, at the same time, it got rid of a number of competitors, who were tiresome if unimportant, without any trouble or bother.

But that is not all. Besides the *irregulars* of whom I have spoken, there has always been a suppressed tendency in criminal circles, as is natural, to escape from the subjection of the Mafia. This tendency came to the surface occasionally in more or less violent forms which were immediately repressed, but it once exploded in a real movement of collective rebellion of which for the moment the criminals had the advantage, the Mafia suffered the shame, and the people, as always, suffered for the damage. It happened in the period immediately after the War. The reason was this. When war was declared, to tell the truth, the evil-doers did not shirk their duty; they went to the front. And in more than one instance men who had till then trodden the ways of evil found on the field of battle the path of redemption. The Mafia, on the contrary, preferred to escape service fraudulently and played the skrimshanker. Moreover, it was able to take all possible advantage of the situation. It grew fat and rich, dressed respectably, declared itself (as well it might) conservative and forgot the past. But the others did not forget. No sooner had they returned from the front, in fact, than the proletarian malefactors regarded the new appearance of the Mafia as a kind of treachery, and, still more, as a source of irritation. And they rose up. They wanted full liberty of action against all, and especially against their ancient chiefs. They let fly—there is no other word for it. Robbery, theft, cattle-raiding, murder, blackmail and every kind of violence were perpetrated, against everything and everybody, as never before. The people, dismayed and bewildered by the suddenness and gravity of the attack, wearily assumed the defensive. But those who had recourse to the constituted authorities, taken unawares and out of their depth, were unable to act. Those who still believed in the omnipotence of the true and greater Mafia and preferred to have recourse to it for protection were often given the answer that it was a serious moment, that they were in a quandary, that there was no more discipline, that the *picciotti* (brigands) had no respect or obedience for any one, and that even the old *mafiosi* themselves—those who had been in command hitherto—had to be on their guard and that, on the whole, there was nothing to be done for the moment. And those who thought they would take direct action—they were very few—got much the worst of it in all but a few cases. So there was nothing left for the populace but to give way and submit to every outrage in silence.

Things were in this state when, in the summer of 1919, the Government of the day sent me to Sicily to put the state of public safety into good order. I had been away for three years, but as soon as I arrived I saw there were two immediate dangers in the situation. The first was that the new criminal forces might, through the evil suggestion of their victorious activity and their easy gains, infect the less resistant elements of the population (especially the young men who formed the majority of it) and districts so far unaffected. The second danger was that, failing any intervention to repress crime, the exasperating activity of the same forces might, quite apart from the huge material damage done, throw the mulcted, discouraged and angry population into the arms of the old Mafia, which was always on the watch and under arms; and thus a new alliance would be formed—naturally, on strict and onerous terms—which, leaving the immorality of the thing out of account, would not have failed in a short space of time to bear its terrible fruits, however salutary its first effect.

It was necessary, therefore, first of all to assert the State's authority immediately by rapid action, which should bring the heart of the people to the side of the Government and, by stifling the unbridled activity of these new criminal forces, to prevent any further contagion or damage. When I proceeded to put my programme of immediate action into practice, I was assailed and almost overwhelmed by a flood of bitter recriminations, curses, complaints, protests and provocations.

There was an outbreak of long-repressed resentment and acute impatience, such as was only to be expected. However, since the execution of the duties entrusted to me in spite of all attempts to thwart them was an undeniable proof of the Government's interest in the conditions of the island, and since, in spite of all, the generous and passionate heart of Sicily asked for nothing better than to believe and hope, people's attitudes began gradually to improve. And so, when the recriminations had ceased, long and painful stories began to come out, of what they had suffered, followed by the first timid confidences and finally in a striking number of instances—a thing which very seldom happens in Sicily where compulsory *omertà*, not the real *omertà*, keeps men's mouths shut—by open denunciations, circumstantial and supported by evidence. That was my first victory.

Being now secure in my rear through the open or concealed assistance of the population and the indirect aid of the injured persons, I passed immediately to the attack, by keeping the active criminals isolated in the worst infested districts, by identifying the different groups, by arresting their members in large numbers and by handing them all over to the judicial authorities on charges of murder, robbery, blackmail, cattle-raiding and so on. Naturally the action that I had to take was adapted to the unbridled activities that it was to suppress: it was rapid and on broad lines, therefore, with sudden strokes made simultaneously at several different places and all decisive in character. The criminal forces were beaten once for all, lost their heads and disappeared bag and baggage, at least for the moment, and the mad access of criminal activity that had been raging in the island ended.

Meanwhile, the Mafia, seeing the rebel forces of crime dispersed, wished to resume absolute command of the situation and make up for its lost time. But it knew perfectly well that my view of things was different. However, a little later, when I was intending to consolidate the results and to take further action, an unexpected task took me 1,200 kilometers away from Sicily in twenty-four hours and kept me absent for some little time. Things then went on in Sicily as they always had. People talked about bringing peace to the country, yielded to pressure and disarmed. For fear of reprisals those who had reported losses or injuries or even given evidence retracted; consequently the cases fell to the ground, the arrested men left prison with the haloes of martyrs and went back to their honest work; and the offences began again, not with the former intensity, but with a normal rhythm, sufficient to make life fairly unbearable, with no guarantee that they would not become acute again in the future. The criminals, on their side, went to Canossa and submitted once more to the Mafia; and the people, as usual, paid for all, while the Mafia reasserted itself more strongly than ever.

And there was another reason for this. At that very time, while men were abandoning themselves, as I have said, to every excess of crime, the so-called *land question* came up and threatened to take a concrete form. This, too, was a post-War phenomenon, but an ancient, natural and legitimate tendency of the Sicilian peasants lay at the heart of it—the tendency to assure themselves, either by full possession or by tenancy, of a piece of land from which to get a livelihood. This tendency, although in the past it had given rise to some trouble and anxiety, held nothing which really constituted a danger of social upheaval or a threat to the rights of property. In fact, it resulted in the formation of rural co-operative societies which sometimes took over the entire purchase, but more often the collective hiring, of large estates: but it had never led to the adoption of any extreme attitudes.

I remember, in this connection, at the time of my first residence in Sicily twenty years ago, that in certain country districts the peasants began to form leagues with the object of obtaining the lease of certain estates. The owners, annoyed and perturbed by the fact that the movement seemed to be led by so-called socialistic elements, were reluctant to agree; and the members of the leagues began going round the estates in large groups, mostly carrying arms, with the object of asserting their authority and of securing, with a little shooting, if necessary, a general abstention from work and the complete abandonment of the farms.

I went to the district one day, accompanied by an officer and some men of the *carabinieri,* to get a personal view of the state of things. Suddenly, as I came out into a broad, deserted valley, I came upon a group of about three hundred leaguers, mostly armed with rifles and mounted. I stopped them and asked them where they were going. They quietly replied that they were going to a certain farm to drive out the personnel and take possession until a definite issue was reached in the negotiations already begun for the lease of land belonging to it. "Is this how you are going!" I exclaimed, pointing to their arms. "Go home," I added, "it will be the better for you."

There was a moment or two of indecision. The peasants looked at one another with questioning looks. Instinctively we gathered up our reins and put our hands to our holsters. Nothing happened.

"We ask nothing better than to go home," those nearest to us said suddenly. "But we must go by a different way to that we came by."

"Why?" I asked. "What has happened?"

"Nothing," they answered. "Only we don't want to cut a poor figure in the eyes of those who sent us."

That was the whole gist of the matter.

Another time, while this movement was in full force, news came of a big meeting of leaguers with the proclaimed intention of proceeding to extremes which was to be held right in the middle of a certain large estate. I went there and found the meeting at its height. In its midst, mounted on a cart, a sort of maniac, dripping with sweat, was braying all kinds of absurdities in a hoarse voice, making havoc of thrones and altars, masters and exploiters of the poor, logic and good sense. It was dreadful. A dense crowd of peasants was standing round the cart with upturned faces, completely stupefied by this avalanche of words they did not understand. Behind these, like a fourfold belt, were several hundred peasants mounted on sturdy mules resignedly toasting themselves in the sun, amid flies and horse-flies, in the name of proletarian rights. Behind these, a fifth belt, were a number of stationary waggons full of women quietly nodding in the suffocating heat.

I went with my men between the waggons, wormed my way in among the rustic cavalry and stood behind the crowd on foot. I listened for a short time. The maniac in the cart was getting shriller and shriller as he approached the social revolution with its usual new dawn. For the moment, however, it was an August afternoon, and burning hot. So, turning to my men, I said in a clear voice: "Boys, I'm going to take the fellow in the cart by the ears and stop him talking. You just look out. If anybody looks nasty, shoot at the mules." The peasants on mules among whom we had wound our way understood me perfectly. Without a word those nearest to us gathered up their reins and prudently moved away: and in a moment the movement spread to the others. "The social revolution will be a fine thing," they no doubt thought, "but it lies beyond the future; but the mules are in the present. A bird in hand is worth two in the bush." And the cavalry forthwith dispersed. The crowd on foot saw no reason for staying, and went away too; while the women in the waggons woke up and ate their lunch. As for the orator, he dried up and vanished at the first signs of dispersal. And this proves that I was right when I said that the ancient and persistent land-hunger of the Sicilian peasants never led to extremes. Agricultural agitation revived, as I said, in the period immediately after the War. There had been so much talk during the War of *land for the fighting men* that the peasants who returned from the battlefield asked for the promise to be fulfilled as soon as they got home. And then a new wave of the old agitation began: there were meetings, groups of demonstrators going round the country, invasions of estates, etc. These demonstrations, in general, though based on rather abstract ideas and often merely symbolic in form, sometimes took on a particular tinge from the reflection of local antagonisms in small country politics. Nothing serious, really: but these were the days when men were talking elsewhere of the Bolshevist movement. This, by repercussion, caused some anxiety in Sicily.

One evening at C-one of the largest landowners in the place came to me very upset. In broken tones and with tears in his eyes he told me that, earlier in the day, two of his farm-hands as they came back from the fields, had seen—so they told him—certain individuals busily measuring the ground.

"They are dividing up my lands!" the poor man sobbed.

"Have no fear, my dear sir," I said to him. "The harvest is in and the land is bare. Don't worry about the men who are measuring it. It is just a way of passing the time, and hurts nobody. We should be in a poor state if it was enough to measure a piece of land to become the owner of it." '

"But these men are in earnest," he answered. "The farms are already occupied by Red Guards!"

I could not set his mind at rest anyhow. So I said: "Very well, I'll go and see to-morrow." And the next morning I went for a tour of the countryside.

The first farm I came to, about ten kilometers from the village, commanded the road from the top of a little hill. It was closed and evidently deserted. On the roof, hanging from a spade-handle stuck up on it, a kind of red rag was fluttering. In front of the door a man was sitting alone; the Red Guard. I called to him. He ran down into the road, recognised me and saluted respectfully.

"What are you doing up there, like a solitary owl?" I asked him.

*"Nente"* (Nothing).

"But aren't you a Red Guard?" *"Accusi dicono"* (So they say). "And what are you guarding?"

*"Nun u sacciu. Mi manàro cca e aspettu ca vennu"* (I don't know. They sent me here and I am waiting for them to come).

"Who?"

*"E ecu u 'sapel A 'eri vinni mi frate a portarmi lu pane"* (How should I know? My brother came to bring me food yesterday).

"And what if nobody comes?"

*"E di chissu mi scantu! Apposta staiu pensannu di jriminni"* (That's just what I'm afraid of. I was just thinking of going away).

"But your post? Your flag? And the revolution?"

*"Un si tratta 'i chissu. Ccà si tratta ca iu restu a dijuno"* (That's not what matters. The question is if I'm to stay here starving).

I couldn't help laughing. The Red Guard plucked up his courage and, coming a little closer, asked: *"Ca dice Voscienza? M'inni vaiu?"* (What does your Honour say? Shall I go away?)

"That is for you to decide, my friend," I answered.

The Last Struggle With The Mafia

My friend scratched the tip of his nose and then said:

*"Ca dice Voscienza? Ne dunano i terre?"* (What does your Honour think? Will they give us the land?)

"If you had a bit of land," I said, "would you let it be taken away from you?"

*"Cissu mai!* (Never!)

"Well then____"

*"Giustu ... m'inni vaiu"* (That's right ... I'm off!). "Good-bye!"

*"Bacio le mani a Voscienza"* (I kiss your Honour's hand).

And so the Red Guard went slowly and quietly off to his distant village, his peaceful hearth and his daily honest toil. And the red flag fluttered harmlessly from the roof of the deserted farm like a peasant's pocket-handkerchief hung out to dry. And from the dreary line of telegraph posts lining the lonely road came an incessant buzz as anxious messages and orders relating to the revolution in progress flashed along the wires.

Two days later, as I was passing in my car along another road in the heart of a district which was said to be one of the most disturbed, I met a group of about a hundred peasants on horseback, the first of whom, riding in front, carried a gorgeous red flag. I drove slowly on amid shying mules and scattered riders until, when I was about halfway through the group, I heard behind me a cry of *'A' bannéra! A' bannéra!"* (The flag!) I must observe that a long tricolour pennon, fixed to the radiator-cap of my car, was fluttering in the wind. I had put it there recently, thinking that a little of the tricolour would look very well with all that red about. The ring of the cry left no room for doubt: they were annoyed at my pennon. I stopped, got out and, turning to the rearguard whence the cry had come, I asked: *"Ca sintite dire cu ste voci?"*

(What do you mean by that cry?) The squadron halted in silence.

*"Ora va'!"* I went on. *"Dicitimi 'na cosa. Quann 'eravu 'n trincea aviavu chissa bannéra o chidda?"* (Come now, tell me something. When you were in the trenches, did you have this flag or that?)

*"Chissa"* (This one), said some of them nodding at the tricolour.

*"E comu fu ca ura canciàstivu di sta manéra?* "(And how is it that you have changed like this, then?), I replied.

There was an awkward silence. A look almost of mortification came into the faces of some. But a hearty young fellow, on the back of a strong and restive mule, came forward and said, in a sharp, clear tone: *"Signuri, chidda* (pointing to the red flag) *"'a portamu pi signali; ma 'nta lu core, sempre chissa avémo"* (Sir, we carry this flag as a signal, but we bear the other always in our hearts). And he pointed with his outstretched arm at the tricolour pennon.

However, all was not a bed of roses. The general mass was rough, impulsive and easily excited, while agitators were not wanting. Besides, one had to reckon with local questions, petty quarrels and personal antagonisms. So that, here and there, there were some excesses and regrettable incidents. And the Mafia took the opportunity to put in its oar and make itself useful—especially to itself by violently suppressing agitators who were infringing its monopoly.

But the situation began getting rapidly calmer owing to peaceful understandings between the peasants and the landowners and to special measures taken by the Government. All the same, there were people who asked what on earth would have happened without the Mafia. And the Mafia proclaimed its good services as maintainer of public order and protector of social peace. Some simple souls believed it; some not quite so simple souls put it about; and the Mafia gained new prestige and new power, when it had already quite enough power in its control of the electoral machine.

To sum up. The special characteristic of crime in Sicily is that it is involved in the machinery of the Mafia. Its prevalence and nature are both conditioned by the qualities in the Sicilian temperament most liable to misapplication—impulsiveness, exuberance, and passion—and, like the Mafia, it diminishes very noticeably as you go from the western and central districts to the eastern district, where large tracts could be found that are quite immune or where only the subtler and more insidious forms of crime prevail. Crime is habitual, tends to combined action, is distinguished by aggressiveness, is dictated by intimidation, and is committed in secret owing to the fact of compulsory *omertà*, its retreat being always assured by popular favour, even though obtained by compulsion, by the custom of providing a sure refuge beforehand and by the ever-open resort to hiding in the vast and solitary estates or in the rocky, deserted hills. The prevalent forms of crime in Sicily are: *robbery*, committed in numbers and armed, preferably in the open country and on the country roads; *blackmail*, either by letter or verbal; *kidnapping*, which was once very frequent but which has now fallen into disuse because, though it often attained its object, it produced little profit and was easily discovered, since it meant the employment of several people, great subdivision of the spoils, frequent quarrels and consequent leakages; *cattle-stealing*, particularly in the shape of big raids, sometimes as an end in itself, but preferably as a means of blackmail; *damage to rural property* (the cutting down of vines, olives, etc.), committed either on a small scale and more as a menace or a threat, or else on a large scale as a personal injury or a vendetta; *bodily injury and homicide*, either in the accomplishment of other crimes (robbery, cattle-stealing, kidnapping, etc.), or for motives of retribution and revenge.

In connection with crimes of bloodshed the complete absence of wounding and homicide in personal strife is to be noted. This is due to the fact that in Sicily one of the most conspicuous sources of quarrels is absent, I mean, the groups of roystering youths that meet at inns, brothels, for singing obscene songs at street-corners or for nocturnal rowdyism: and there are also no mixed gatherings of people in which both sexes share easily in more or less free forms of amusement. The Sicilian of the people, sober, quiet and a respecter of tradition, amuses himself in the family or in a group of families; he does not like promiscuity or amusements open to all, and, even when he gets warmed up, he knows how to amuse himself without falling into excess, and without forgetting the respect due to himself and to his neighbour. As for the young men, in certain cases they prefer to be alone; but when they are in a company they do not quarrel or make a noise. They do not drink, and, if in the high spirits of youth or under the enchantment of the evening air laden with the scent of orange-blossom and broom they burst into song, they raise their voices in slow and melancholy dirges, or sing songs with choruses to the sound of mandolines and guitars.

Public brawling is relegated to low women and low streets, for the Sicilian, especially the peasant, is not a talker; he is, rather, taciturn and reserved, and, when insulted, has no need to work himself up with cries. He either takes immediate action or, as more often happens, he reserves it for the proper time and place.

The last characteristic, and one specially remarkable, is the frequency of crimes, especially those involving bloodshed, committed out of revenge. In Sicily, where the sun is fiery and men's hearts are fiery too, every feeling is passionate and every insult is paid for. Moreover, the memory of an injury does not fade in course of time; it grows intenser: and for that reason alone vendetta seems to be excessive and out of all proportion to the initial, distant motive. Vendetta, in Sicily, does not immediately follow the injury, as a rule: it waits, watches and spies, for long years if need be, until the favourable moment when, either through the lapse of time or intervening events, its author will not be suspected. Then, suddenly, unexpectedly and anonymously, it comes down like the wrath of God, while its agent, alone and wrapped in a veil of mystery, takes the bitter yet doubly sweet satisfaction into the recesses of his heart. But if a question of personal honour is involved, then vendetta must be, and is always, immediate, ostentatious and as public as the fulfilment of a sacred duty. One may accuse the Sicilians of having too touchy natures, and of being slaves of tradition; but it must not be forgotten that for many generations the absence of legal protection made private vengeance seem nothing more than justice.

# Typical Figures

The characteristics of crime in Sicily, described in the last chapter, lead to special difficulties in prevention, in discovery and in the identification of offenders and their accomplices and in proving individual guilt. To bring the guilty to justice presents no fewer difficulties, but it is essential to the assertion of the State's power and authority, and is particularly important and effective, not only as an end in itself completing repressive action, but as a measure calculated to strike at the prestige and prevalence of crime, to reduce its intimidatory power over injured parties and witnesses, and to prevent the crimes associated with *latitanza*, i.e. those to which the criminals wanted by the police have recourse either to secure the necessities of life or to ensure their liberty. The difficulty lies in the elusiveness of criminals in Sicily and in their habitual concealment. Undiscoverability is the normal state of criminals on the island: but with this special qualification that, whereas criminals in all countries tend to be undiscoverable, and for a good reason, the criminal in Sicily has not only the habit, but also the science, of eluding discovery.

The Sicilian criminal, even when he has not committed an offence, or is not thinking of committing one at the moment, is above all an undiscoverable person in his contacts with justice. When he is looked for, even on the most innocent grounds, he is not to be found. You do not even catch a glimpse of him. If you *do* meet him, it is invariably at a cross-roads where there are at least two ways of retreat open. He salutes you if he is at least twenty yards off; at a smaller distance he turns about, so that if a race has to be run, he has a good long start. He never goes in front of the agents of public safety: he follows them. He has a way of entering his own house by the window, and he often goes out of the door—somebody else's door.

This last device was so evidently useful that I often adopted it myself. At times when the fight was particularly warm and rapid surprises were highly necessary, when I could only succeed by concealing my movements from the close spying of the evildoers, I was sometimes seen to come to a friend's house late in the afternoon, with the mild aspect that the occasion demanded and in the most innocent garb—a tail coat, walking shoes, a bowler hat, a cane and such like, as though for a game of bridge. Nobody suspected that the same night I went out by a back window in a velvet jacket, riding boots, *coppola* (cap), Winchester rifle, and such like, including the attribute of being ubiquitous that was assigned to me.

The Sicilian criminal is very difficult to find at home after dark; if he is there, he is not in bed, but underneath it. He prefers to sleep by day and to be awake at night, like the watch-dogs by whose friendship, naturally, he sets great store. If he sees that he is being watched, he disappears completely for at least three days; if you send for him, he disappears for at least a week, and in his place comes somebody with whom you have nothing to do, in order to find out what is going on. Sometimes, however, when he is far from your thoughts, you may see him pass quite close to you with a deep bow. That is a bad sign.

It means that he has been up to one of his little games. His meeting with you will serve as a proof of the *alibi* he has already arranged. Which shows that the classical axiom about the guilty running away is relative.

Then there is the undiscoverability of the criminal in a specific case. As soon as a crime has been committed, all its authors, accessories and accomplices become immediately undiscoverable. And not only they, but a large number of other people who have nothing to do with the crime, but who feel a well-justified anxiety, that is, the ex-criminals most likely to have done the deed and the criminals who are relations, friends or acquaintances of the guilty ones. Even that is not the whole number who disappear.

One must add to them other criminals who, although they had nothing to do with the crime, and no particular reasons for anxiety connected with it, disappear in the thought that, after all, when justice gets going over a new crime, anybody who has old scores with it, whether paid or not, might just as well take a change of air.

The general and precautionary state of undiscoverability special to crime in Sicily is thus divided into two elements: the *latitanti* (men in hiding) and the *irreperibili* (undiscoverables). The *latitanti* are individuals for whose arrest warrants have been issued by the judicial authorities for proved responsibility for a given crime and who have escaped arrest. They try to keep themselves hidden until the revocation of the warrant, either through lapse of the proceedings or their acquittal, with the prospect of having to remain undiscoverable indefinitely when the preliminary examination and the trial result in their conviction. The *irreperibili* are men who have gone voluntarily into hiding, but are not wanted by the police, either because they are guilty of crimes unknown to the authorities because not reported, or because they are the unidentified authors of reported crimes, or because of anxiety due to having personal relations with criminals, or to general considerations. All these remain in secure hiding till the end of the preliminary examination, but may remain so indefinitely where, through a continuous succession of crimes, their motives of anxiety become indefinitely multiplied and superimposed.

Some idea, although largely approximate, of this phenomenon may be derived from a few[r] figures that refer, of course, to bygone times. In view of the Sicilian criminal's habit of acting in numbers, the average number of authors of any crime may be taken as three, so that for a hundred crimes there would be nominally three hundred guilty persons. I say *nominally*, because, owing to the prevalence of repeated crime, a certain number of crimes are committed by the same persons. So that, putting the average number of crimes committed by the same individual at three, it follows that the number of those effectively guilty of a hundred crimes under review would not be three hundred but one hundred. As I have already said, not all crimes are reported to the authorities. Let us therefore put the number of those one hundred crimes that come to the knowledge of the authorities, either directly or by report, at eighty. In view of the difficulty of inquiry, the authorities, on the most favourable presumptions, only succeed in finding the authors of half the crimes that come to their knowledge. So, in this case, the number will be forty, with the identification of forty culprits. Of these forty culprits, it may be calculated that twenty are immediately brought to justice. The other twenty escape immediate arrest, and become undiscoverable; meanwhile warrants are issued for their arrest and they become *latitanti* in the classical sense of the word. Simultaneously, the following have become undiscoverable: the persons guilty of the twenty out of the one hundred crimes committed but unknown to the authorities, i.e. twenty; those guilty of the forty crimes known to the authorities but of which they do not know the authors, i.e. forty; the criminals who have had no share in the hundred crimes committed, but who are relations, friends or acquaintances of the culprits, in all (reckoning an average of two per culprit) two hundred; the most likely ex-criminals (the so-called "black sheep" in the current phrase) to be wanted for that particular crime, whom we will number x, it being impossible to give even an approximate figure for them; the persons who take general precautions, i.e. those criminals who although they had no share in the crimes committed, think they had better keep out of the way, and we will call them y. So that, as the consequence of the first hundred crimes in any year, there will be at least, to begin with, *arrested* 20; *undiscoverable* 20 (*latitanti*), + 200 + x + y.

The final arithmetic of this state of things depends mainly on three factors: the length of the legal proceedings, the intensity of the criminal action and the efficiency of the police. Except for possible variation due to the attitude or action of the police, the anxieties which gave rise to the initial undiscoverability remain substantially the same till judicial action is concluded. What the authorities think of the matter becomes certain (to some extent) or, at all events, becomes known with the ending of the preliminary examination. Then, and only then, can anyone decide what to do. And since the average length of the penal examinations (I speak of past times, for the Fascist Government has given proof of surprising quickness in this matter) was two years, one can only get an idea of the situation by taking the intensity of criminal activity, that is, the number of times in the course of two years the hundred crimes were repeated—and in the light of statistics it was not a few times—and compute the numerical consequences in the way of *latitanza* and simple *irreperibilità*. The only reduction in that sum would be due to a small percentage caused by repeated crime, which means an aggravation of personal guilt but a diminution of the number of culprits.

The action of the police was always characterised, especially in the suppression of *latitanza*, by vigour and personal courage. Ample evidence of heroism on the part of our police force—the officials and agents of public security, the Royal Carabinieri and the young voluntary Militia of Public Safety—exists, but they could not sensibly improve the situation. Owing to the incongruities of the old criminal procedure which excessively hampered initiative and movement, to defects of organisation, to insufficient means, and to such special adverse conditions as difficult ground, favouring of criminals and traditional, compulsory *omertà*, the prehensile capacity of the police could not keep pace with the continual increase of crime. Indeed, the number of *latitanti* and undiscoverables increased in time to such an extent that it could only be arrived at after complicated and tiresome calculations: but I think I have said enough on the point.

I will only add that this increase brought about: on one hand, a notable increase of clandestine emigration with a proportionate development and perfection of the trade in false passports and other dishonest activities depending on it; and on the other hand, especially in the country, a particular state of existence in which the impossibility of stable occupation, implicit for reasons of safety in *latitanza* and generally in *irreperibilità*, necessarily imposed a life of complete parasitism on *latitanti* and *irreperibili* (apart from their evil instincts), and forced the rural population to adapt itself and submit to it as to an unavoidable tribute. In fact, in the budgets of certain agricultural undertakings a certain sum was set apart for this payment, without prejudice to the so-called *taglie* (taxes) of which I shall speak later. It is unnecessary to say that the common and continual presence of these elements in the country was a powerful factor in aggravating the dangerousness of a neighbourhood, in depressing the *morale* of the population and in accentuating obligatory *omertà* and compulsory harbouring of criminals.

In the distant, solitary and boundless tracts of the *latifondi* and in the deserted mountains, the movement of the *latitanti* and the *irreperibili* hinged principally on the *campieri* and took place almost openly and without hindrance in the light of day. In the neighbourhood of inhabited centres the movement was subterranean, coming up to the surface at night or before dawn; but it had its periscope, the *capraio* (goatherd), a figure worthy of illustration. Sometimes the goatherd was an honest fellow; but in that case he could not escape the common law; he had no luck and did not last long. As a rule the goatherd was a *mafioso* and a thorough bad lot. Owning a flock of goats, the origin of which it would have been indiscreet and certainly useless to inquire into, he derived his apparent livelihood from selling milk, which he delivered at the door, bringing the favoured goat even up to the top floor and setting the women quarrelling about the measure he gave. So, at least in appearance, he earned his living. As for the goats, he maintained them by feeding them on other men's land, so scientifically, so persistently and so widely that he became looked on as a regular scourge of the fields nearest to a village.

The peasants were afraid of him and hated him fiercely, and he returned their feelings with interest, so that bloody incidents occurred in which the goatherd sometimes got the worst of it:

in other words, he was laid out with a couple of bullets in him. But in these cases the jury, on some such ground as legitimate self-defence, no intent to kill, serious provocation or mental deficiency would simply convict the murderer of carrying dangerous weapons or some other minor offence that might be considered cancelled by a short sentence of imprisonment. And that was simple justice.

The attempts of the rural administrations to put a check on abusive pasturage by goatherds were therefore particularly characteristic. I have seen certain rural police regulations which were a perfect mass of subtleties. There was an obligation to have a special licence to exercise a goatherd's calling, another obligation to show his contracts for pasturage, another to leave a village by certain fixed roads, to come in again by other roads, to go to the pasturage by fixed paths, prohibition from moving at certain hours, from staying in certain places, from joining company with any others, etc., etc. And I have seen a magistrate new to the country look aghast at these regulations, in the name of the law and constitution, and be surprised when I smiled, as though I was displaying an indifference to judicial probity.

Taken literally, of course, these regulations would have left nothing for a goatherd to do but hang himself on the nearest tree. But the goatherds found their own way out of the difficulty. They bowed deeply to the mayor; they waited patiently in the waiting-rooms of the competent officials; they regularly provided themselves with all the papers, permits, stamps, etc., prescribed; they signed all the affidavits, obligations and prohibitions with beautiful crosses; they slipped a lira or two into the usher's hand, they saluted the guard, they took their goats—and they did exactly what they pleased.

The goatherd, a born observer with a perfect topographical knowledge of the villages and the country round them, from being continually on the go between them, was the natural hyphen between the *latitanti* and *irreperibili* who were hiding outside and their parents and friends who lived in the village. He was not only their periscope, but their wireless and their telephone too. If need be, he would also undertake postal duties, such as carrying letters, preferably fraudulent ones, or diplomatic errands such as taking messages—demands, intimidations, threats and the like—all except those of gallantry with which nobody entrusted him, since he was capable of translating them into action himself. Above all, the goatherd was a news-gatherer. He would absorb news in a village like a sponge and squeeze it out into the innermost recesses of the countryside, for the benefit of the *latitanti* and others, as he drove his flock to more or less forbidden pastures: at the same time he absorbed news in the country and squeezed it out in the village, there being no corner and no family in a village to which he did not find his way on the good pretext of selling milk. He was a splendid sponge, except where the authorities and the police were concerned. For them he squeezed out nothing, but only absorbed. And in order to do this with greater success, he would make eyes at the maids in the barracks of the Carabinieri, the judge's maid, the maid of the Commissary of Public Security, the police-sergeant's maid, and so on.

He would heave a great sigh, shoot a fiery glance and out with a "Signorina *bedda (bella)*" How could the girl be rude to a great upstanding fellow who looked at her like that and said *"Signorina bedda"* even if she was fifty years old, had a squint and was rather hump-backed? Sometimes the woman—especially if she belonged to the place—although flattered, knew or guessed the little game and the character of its player and was not taken in; but more often she fell into the trap. Then her mistress would intervene with:

"Philomena, why don't you stop playing the fool with the goatherd?"

"But what is the harm, *signora?*"

"What? Don't you know he's been in prison for theft, assault and all sorts of things?"

"Perhaps, but you wouldn't think so to talk to him. He's so good-mannered and so respectful to the master. He is always asking after him."

That is what went on. By means of little indiscretions picked up in this way the goatherd succeeded in getting to know or in guessing everything that was going on in the neighbourhood of the authorities and the police, so as to communicate it conscientiously to all his country friends. But the goatherd, like all poisons in the world, had, or should have had, his specific antidote in the *guardia campestre* (field watchman), a typical institution and a man specially entrusted with the duty of seeing that local police regulations in the country were carried out. The *guardia campestre*, where he exists today, is a communal police agent like any other, who carries out his duties with self-sacrifice, discipline and correctness: often he is an ex-soldier who brings the prestige of a blue ribbon[8] to the execution of his duties. In former times, however, things were different. The post of *guardia campestre*, held in reserve as a prize for voters, was conferred on men whom the communal administration entrusted with the duties, and who served the community as a kind of faithful Pretorian guard.

In the exercise of their functions these *guardie campestri* had a particular, traditional mentality, which can only be explained by reference to the past, and to the earliest forms of police-organisation in Sicily. The earliest form of local police in Sicily was the so-called *Capitani d'armi*, first established in 1543. There were three of these Captains of Arms, each with ten mounted men, and they were supposed to provide for the public security of the island. They were few in number and of doubtful material, if we may judge from old documents of the various abuses of their power with which they were charged, especially

8    i.e. the ribbon of the medal for military valour

that of demanding complete maintenance and lodging for themselves, their men and their horses from the country people and of so arbitrarily and frequently requisitioning horses that people preferred to keep no horses at all to avoid vexation.

This system lasted for some time, till in 1583, under the Viceroy Marco Antonio Colonna, the first complete regulations were issued for the " *Captains of Arms deputed to put down bandits*" by which each of the three captains was given a company of thirty mounted arquebusiers. But the new regulations did not entirely rectify the abuses, especially since they provided for the appointment of "extraordinary Captains of Arms" in emergencies: and these abuses, particularly those committed by the extraordinary Captains of Arms, grew so serious as to end in a regular combination between them and the criminals at the expense of the unhappy rural population. One of their specialities was false accusation by anonymous letter against honest and well-to-do farmers. These accusations, transmitted by the unconscious higher authorities to the very Captains of Arms who had been responsible for sending them in, led either to blackmail or, in cases of resistance, to judicial persecution by the aid of false witnesses provided by the Captains of Arms themselves.

As time went on, the obligation to make good from their own property thefts committed in territory under their jurisdiction was imposed upon the Captains of Arms. The intention was good and might have led to satisfactory results, as it did in Sardinia after the institution of the *barraccelli;* but in practice it proved dangerous, because those who formed part of the Companies of Arms in Sicily observed it either by compelling persons who had suffered robbery not to report their losses, but to negotiate with the thieves for the recovery of their property, or by making good losses incurred in their territory by the spoils of robberies committed for the purpose in other places.

This obligation to make losses good was maintained in all the transformations that the special body of police underwent until its suppression in 1877. In 1813 the extraordinary Captains of Arms were done away with, and the number of Companies of Arms was increased to twenty-three, with a special uniform and regulations. In 1837 the Companies of Arms were done away with and a *gendarmeria reale a cavallo* (royal horse gendarmerie) was instituted in Sicily, composed of ten squadrons into which all the details of the old Companies of Arms were drafted. In 1860 these gendarmes of the Bourbon regime were replaced by the *Militi a cavallo per la sicurezza interna* (horse soldiers for internal security), recruited from the second category of the national militia, and organised in sections of thirty men for each district, Palermo having two sections. The names and uniforms were changed; but the traditional mentality of the corps remained what it was, especially owing to the inconveniences that arose under the obligation to make good losses by theft and cattle-raiding, and by the presence in the new corps of many ancient elements.

Then came the great surprise, called the surprise of the *tre munzedda* (three heaps). At the beginning of 1877 the Government of the day sent the prefect Malusardi to restore order in the very troubled conditions of public security. Malusardi at once saw how injurious the existing organisation was and what were the methods of the corps of native police. One fine day all the *militi a cavallo* in Sicily were summoned to Palermo for an inspection. They were divided, when they assembled, into three groups (the *tre munzedda*). One group, formed of the best men, was retained for service; another group, formed of undesirables, was relieved of its duties, uniform and arms, and sent home; the third group, formed of the real ruffians, was immediately disarmed and sent *en bloc* to a compulsory domicile. The execution of the Royal Decree of March 27th, 1877, dissolved the corps of *militi a cavallo*, and substituted for it a corps of *guardie di pubblica sicurezza a cavallo*, into which was drafted the first of the above-mentioned three groups and which formed part of the *guardie di pubblica sicurezza* of the kingdom. The new State police was thus inaugurated in Sicily with the corps of Royal Carabinieri which was national in character and the corps of *guardie di pubblica sicurezza* which was regional in character. But in course of time the idea of having a regional police for Sicily died out and the police organisation took on a completely national character, with the *carabinieri reali* on the one hand, and the *guardie di pubblica sicurezza*, later the *guardie di città*, subsequently the *guardia regia*, and finally the *Agenti di pubblica sicurezza* on the other. To-day the organisation is both national and Fascist, with the gallant assistance of the voluntary militia.

The remaining elements of the regional State police that had been abolished were either reabsorbed in their localities (and not always by the best localities) or passed—often at urgent request—into the communal police, in the shape of *guardie campestri,* bringing with them as relics of the mentality and the traditional practice of the older corps a certain tendency to smooth things over, to compromise and to ambiguity such as to create the suspicion, often wrongly, that they had a foot in both camps. Not a few of them, indeed, were excellent fellows. As for their duty, they did it, often with good results and even with a display of courage and personal valour: but they had their own ideas of how it ought to be done.

Being perfectly acquainted with the neighbourhood, the men, the affairs and the geography, and first-class investigators, up to all the tricks of the trade and conversant with the psychology of crime, they were called in to help the State police, preferably in desperate cases or when it was desired to mask the objectives, aims and movements of the authorities. Then, on the pretext of asking their advice or by giving them the illusion of having found out secrets, they were told elaborate lies in the hope, not always vain, that they would divulge them. Their services were then very useful, if misdirected. I had experience of this on the occasion of my first experience of elections.

An electoral struggle was at fever heat in one of the communes of the island. A ballot was to be held, to the results of which the prefecture attached great importance. As usual, the two candidates accused one another of influencing the electors through the Mafia or criminal agencies; but the man who sounded this note loudest was the candidate favoured by the political authorities. As a matter of fact, both availed themselves of the Mafia and criminal agencies to a varying extent of which we had no means of judging. However, on the Saturday morning preceding the ballot, I was ordered to go to the spot to ensure public order and the liberty of voting, which was seriously threatened by some malefactors acting on behalf of the opposing candidate: and I was provided with an interminable list of these so that I might have something to go upon and, above all, so that I might take timely measures to remove them from circulation with the intent to avoid regrettable incidents. "Prevent, always prevent,"

I was told: "Never suppress." "Exactly," I thought to myself. "Prevention is everything in this game, and suppression useless. Once a vote is given, it is given." And off I went.

But the job of prevention, that is of removing them from circulation in good time, was too much for me: I could not have done it. The list was long, and the possibility that some of the electors might be in it could not be excluded. And time pressed. I decided, therefore, on my line of action. When I reached the village, I told the local police officer to make some pretext for calling to the office the *guardia campestre* in whom he had least confidence. The man came and, when the suitable moment arrived, I took care to let him hear me tell the official to employ him in looking up in the archives and preparing the personal *dossiers* of all the people mentioned in the famous list, which I openly handed to him. "We'll talk about it to-night," I concluded, with my most gloomy smile: and then I went off to lunch.

The consequences of my action were automatic and certain. No sooner had he prepared the *dossiers* than the *guardia campestre* would hasten to warn all those interested and they would spontaneously and hastily leave the village till the voting was over. My object would be attained without any further action.

That is exactly what happened, and the next day, in spite of all prophecies to the contrary, there was perfect peace and the voting went off quickly and quietly. But the joke was against me, for—when the numbers were read out, the candidate favoured by the authorities was beaten.

The reason was this. The *guardia campestre,* who clearly had little sympathy for our candidate, had certainly, as I had foreseen, warned all the persons on the list; but on his own account he had hastened to do the same to those who were not on the list. During the evening, therefore, the malefactors left the place *en masse:* so that, when it came to voting, the man who had the largest number on his side came off worst. Perhaps it was the finger of Providence!

Substantially, therefore, the old *guardie campestri* were distrusted, as an insidious danger to the organisation of the State police. The distrust was often unjust or exaggerated: for it was forgotten that these men, apart from all other considerations, belonged to the locality, were men of the people with family, relations, friends and interests there and therefore, by this very fact, rather hampered in their actions. In such conditions they ought not to have been asked to give more than they could. On the other hand, they themselves admitted the difficulty. More than once, when police operations were pending, I have heard one of the old *guardie campestri* say: "If you are going to do anything affecting such and such a family, let me off duty and tell me nothing about it: I don't want to know." And he would go away, without speaking to anyone, into the country for a few days and stay there till the business was over, showering summonses for contravening the regulations on the goatherds of the party in opposition to the communal administration.

One of the most characteristic traits of these men was their contempt for the penal and judicial system in force which they considered quite inadequate for the fight against crime. Evidently they had inherited a trace of the spirit that inspired the ancient *bandi* (edicts) which punished with death even the smallest theft, and at the first offence. They had an insuperable distrust and dislike for everything that had to do with scientific police work. Yet, when given a job and left to carry it out in their own way, they could do it.

Once, in a case of nocturnal attack on a house, certain police officials who had come to the spot were trying to pack safely in a box the glass chimney of a paraffin lamp on which there were finger-marks which might assist in the rather difficult investigations. An old *guardia campestre* was assisting in the operation, with an ironic wrinkle at the corner of his mouth, and, at a certain moment, he shrugged his shoulders and went out. I saw him shortly afterwards in the rustic courtyard of the house intently scrutinising the chalky ground which was dotted all over with hoof-marks of all kinds of animals. I asked him what he was doing, and he answered that while *they* (the officers with the lamp chimney) were bothering themselves unnecessarily about a few human finger-marks, he thought it was better to pay attention to the marks of certain horses' hoofs. I looked at him with surprise, because to find a definite track in that muddy tangle of hoof-marks made by horses, cows and sheep seemed to me impossible. Nevertheless, the *guardia campestre* came to tell me, a little later, that one of the aggressors was undoubtedly riding a mule lame in the off hind leg. He had been able, in that tangle of tracks, to single out the mark of a mule-shoe finished with two strips of iron of different lengths, obviously so made to correct a defect in the animal's off hind hoof. How he had managed to do this I have no idea, because, apart from the number, nature and confusion of the tracks in the mud of the yard, the two strips of iron left no mark on the surface, but only in depth. All the same, the facts proved that the man was right.

He was a very curious type, and he spoke for preference in aphorisms. On the occasion of an animal fair he was once sent with other agents of police to watch one of the roads leading to the fair. As a large herd of animals went by, the head of the patrol asked the men who were with it to show the documents called *bollette* that were then in use to prove the legitimate ownership of the animals. All brought them out, except one old peasant who could produce none and gave the excuse that he had lost them. Another, however, showed a mass of documents, more numerous than his animals, with the explanation that in his haste he had taken up some documents that had expired. The head of the patrol was ordering, as seemed logical, that the old man without papers should be stopped and the rest allowed to go on, when the *guardia campestre,* shaking his head, said: "An honest man may well have no papers; but a thief will certainly have too many." The head of the patrol did not take offence, but had another look: the *guardia campestre* was right. The old peasant without a *bolletta* went on his way, while the man who had too many stayed with the police. He had a reserve of old *bollette* which, with some unnoticeable retouching could have very well served at the fair to justify the possession of other people's animals.

Another time, the same *guardia campestre* was going along with me and some other police agents on a tour of inspection of certain country districts where a band of unknown young ruffians was committing a number of thefts and robberies. At a certain point, where the lane turned a corner, we came on a youth who looked rather dishevelled and disturbed. I told him to stop and I questioned him about himself and his reasons for being where he was. Although he stumbled a little in his speech (which might well have been due to natural fright) he came out of it pretty well. Suddenly the *guardia campestre* got off his horse, came slowly up to the lad I was questioning and looking him in the face said: "Spit."

The lad put on a forced smile. "There's nothing to laugh about," said the *guardia,* and he repeated: "Spit." This time the lad obeyed: he made a face, tried to spit but nothing happened. His tongue was obviously dry, as sometimes happens when a person is caught wrongdoing. *"Cavalere"* the old *guardia* then said to me, *"portamunillu ca è megghiu"* (we'd better take him along with us). A little later the lad was recognised by some of the victims of the robbery as one of the authors of the offences committed in the neighbourhood.

One day I was making some melancholy observations on the large number of criminals, the number of crimes committed, the duties of the police, and so on. Perhaps I was depressed: anyhow the old *guardia campestre* who was present felt he ought to cheer me up and he did it in his own way. "There must be thieves," he said. "If there were no thieves there'd be no merit in being an honest man. The police have nothing to do with it. The police are the telescope the Government keeps for the public to see what's going on with. And so, according to circumstances, it gives it 'em right way up or wrong way up!"

All in all, although I know all their defects and their odd way of looking at things, I have very happy memories of these old *guardie campestri*. I have often been conscious of their suppressed reaction against evil, beneath their ambiguous attitudes. And I can never forget that, among the many officials and agents of public security and officers and men of the *carabinieri* who were my comrades in some rather nasty moments there were also some of these humble *guardie campestri*.

Another typical figure in this connection is the *campiere* on whom, as I have already said, hinged the movements of the *latitanti* and *irreperibili* in general in the districts of the large estates. The *campiere* fulfils the functions of a watchman on agricultural estates, both on the owner's account as against the *gabellotti*, or tenants, and on account of both landlord and tenants as against evildoers. He is a typical local institution and has remote origins also. In distant times, under the regime of the barons, he was something akin to the *bravo*, and he preserved this kinship, in a more or less modified form, even down to our own times, in large landed properties, where the feudal mentality persisted longest. I have found traces of this descent in the fact that some old *campieri* wore only one spur, "only *cavalieri* (gentlemen) having the right to wear both spurs," as they told me.

Since he arose through the necessity of providing directly for the protection of landed property—especially of *latifondi*—which was particularly exposed to the attacks of criminals and was left undefended, where it was not actually exploited, by the famous Companies of Arms, the *campiere* could not have a too saintly character.

Left alone in the distant and dangerous solitudes of the huge estates, in continual contact with evildoers by whom he had to make himself respected, the *campiere*, so long as landed property had to provide for its own defence, had necessarily to be a tried man, ready for all emergencies and capable above all of asserting his personal superiority: he had, therefore, to be not only a man of stout heart, but also a *mafioso*. One only of these two qualities would not have been enough. A *campiere* who was not a *mafioso*, however brave he might have been, would have brought all kinds of troubles on the property entrusted to his care and, in any case, he would have been overpowered by mere numbers: while a *campiere* who was not particularly courageous, though a *mafioso* of the deepest dye, would have been "got round," even in the best of circumstances. Therefore, there was no choice for the landowners: and *campiere* abounded. Although they were often faithful and conspicuously honest towards their own employers, and capable even of risking their lives in bringing safely back to the village the often considerable sums they had collected in rent, they were also capable of playing them the dirtiest tricks. Indeed, there were not wanting instances where the landowners were kidnapped and held to ransom at the inspiration, and even with the personal assistance, of these very *campieri* whom they paid to protect their rights and clothed in a special livery. As for the property entrusted to their care, the *campieri* guaranteed its safety above all by the personal prestige which they enjoyed among the Mafia and the evildoers—and this was more valuable than several dozen muskets for the purpose. But they dealt with petty criminals who were working on their own account and in no organisation by shooting them.

In regard to the Mafia and evildoers in general their motto, quite seriously, was: "No interference here," which was the same as saying: "No interference where I am"; and this not only meant: "Do what you like anywhere else," but also: "If you want help, call on me." Which will make it comprehensible both what a net of complications was caused in the large estates by reciprocal interests and how many motives existed for quarrelling among the *campieri*. These quarrels were either settled in bloody encounters or, more usually, by injurious acts such as large thefts of cattle, serious damage to crops, etc., in which, if the *campiere* suffered the insult, the owner suffered the loss.

In the melancholy solitude that hangs over him, the *campieri's* feeling for the open country is that of the sailor for the sea or of the Bedouin for the desert: he hears its innumerable secret and mysterious voices, he knows its surprises, he interprets all its aspects and on them bases his prophecies. Being accustomed to wide spaces, he sees a long way; and being continually threatened by hidden danger, he sees everything. And he knows everything, especially what cannot be seen. When he is at his post, he never speaks to anyone for any reason: he watches, listens and acts accordingly, never divulging his thoughts to a soul, never getting excited and never seeming to be in a hurry. He keeps his horse at a walk and moves forward at the same easy uniform pace whether he is taking his horse to drink or whether he is going to some appointed spot with the intention of ridding himself of a troublesome thief or a redoubtable enemy. He keeps a certain contact with the village, to which however he seldom comes down, his chief visits being at the time of the seasonal fairs at which the buying and selling of cattle is a traditional pretext for gatherings of the rural Mafia.

The *campiere* is undoubtedly a man of a particular temperament and some places in the island specialise in producing them. Since the office arose as it did, it was not long before the Mafia monopolised its functions to its own purposes. The right of choice being denied to the landowners, the *campieri* were imposed on them individually by the Mafia. By this means the Mafia not only found remunerative employment for many of its most active and resolute members, but could distribute them conveniently about the island so that, on the one hand, it could hold the landed interests in more complete subjection and, on the other, it had an organised system of well-tried adherents on which the whole movement of rural crime could turn, especially as regards the safety in general of *latitanti* and *irreperibili,* the great mass of whom it took care to keep under its thumb so as to prevent any action that might endanger the intricate system of crime and to further its own interests and prestige. On the other hand, *latitanti* and *campieri* had too many opportunities of injuring one another not to understand the convenience of being on good terms. The result can easily be imagined. Not only was large landed property (even when held by some kind of co-operative ownership) completely under the thumb of the Mafia, but, under the system by which it chose the *campieri,* an impenetrable protective network woven in one piece was thrown over *latitanti* and criminals of every kind, and there grew up the general practice of harbouring and receiving by pre-arrangement which was the principal *point d'appui* of the boldest robberies and cattle-raids that did so much harm to the agricultural interests of the island. This system, like some huge oesophagus, was capable of absorbing dozens of waggons of grain stolen on the roads and thousands of heads of cattle of every kind stolen anywhere. The full force of its suction was felt in the districts of the large estates, and its power was increased by the closed frontiers between the provinces. Indeed, it often occurred that these provincial frontiers, for reasons of territorial jurisdiction, created such a solution of continuity in State action that they became the securest lines of transit for the activities of crime, since, to cross them freely, it was good enough to see that a competent *campiere* gave the order or the signal.

# The Latitante

The phenomenon of *latitanza* (hiding), as a particularly dangerous form of criminal life, as a danger specific to the country districts and as an open proof of the insufficiency of the legal power, has always caused great anxiety in Sicily, greater anxiety sometimes than that roused by the frequency of crime itself. There are traces of this in the old edicts against outlaws and bandits, *forusciti, banditi, forgtudicati, discorritori di campagna,* etc., and against all who harboured or helped them, or even against those who merely accompanied them. There was, for instance, the *bando delle teste,* under which a criminal who gave to justice, alive or dead, a bandit guilty of more serious crimes than he himself had committed escaped his penalty. And if the person who delivered up the bandit alive or dead was guilty of no crime, he had the right to obtain exemption from punishment for an offender designated by himself, so long as the offender was guilty of lesser crimes than the bandit's. And a regular case law grew up on the subject. But *latitanza* maintained the upper hand: it survived its hard times and reached our own day in a state of perfect efficiency, helped by the wide meshes in the net of penal procedure; it became so general that by its means not a few occasional offenders became habitual criminals.

The *latitante* holds a privileged position in the criminal world. The warrant for his arrest confers rights on him and allows him more or less poetic licences which are denied to those who have not attained the proud honour of being wanted by the police. But distinctions must be drawn, for there are various kinds of *latitanti.* There is the man who is simply hiding to escape the police and limits his activities to what are simply necessary for existence or for safety. He is not therefore particularly dangerous and is more often rather an occasional offender than a true criminal. But there are *latitanti* who find in their condition power and opportunity for the greater development of their ordinary criminal activities; and there are others who make it a starting-point for special activities. These two kinds are true *latitanti*. The first are common *latitanti*, mass productions and very numerous, so that they are accustomed to traffic and mingle with the free criminals; the others are high-class *latitanti*, hand-finished articles, and therefore few in number, solitary and reluctant to join with others below their own class and stature, except to command them. It is among these last that the bandits are to be found, i.e. *latitanti* who, owing to the extreme gravity of their crimes or the heaviness of their sentences or through indomitable instinct, have placed themselves irremediably outside the law and the civil community. As for the so-called *brigand*, he is not necessarily a *latitante:* he may also be a free criminal. Brigandage is a typical crime in rural districts, highly intensified and preferably exercised in bodies and as a trade. As such, at least in its higher and classic forms, it never had a very noticeable development in Sicily, where the *latitante* throve in every way and banditry had many notable figures.

A characteristic form of *latitanza* is the *armed band*, which is a wandering group of armed *latitanti*, mounted for preference, continually prowling up and down the countryside. In earlier days there was a large number of these bands in Sicily, well organised and trained, who gave much trouble to the police; but in recent years they decayed and only a few sporadic instances were left. The less important ones, reduced to four or five men on foot, were content with a very narrow zone of influence: others, more important, like the band of the Madonie of whom I shall speak later, became sedentary; they were scattered about in the villages with the necessary precautions, ready to collect and mount their horses from time to time for particular enterprises or for mere tours of inspection. Naturally, the armed bands were composed of *latitanti* of quality and bandits. They were formed either by spontaneous mutual attraction or through common needs of life, self-protection and action, and they lived by continual blackmail, occasional depredation and above all by *taglie*. The *taglie* were fixed tributes imposed on individual landowners in proportion to their capacity to pay, and they sometimes amounted (with liability to increase in cases of default) to the considerable sums of ten, twenty or even fifty thousand lire a year. A regular accounting system, with proper ledgers, existed for them.

Generally, every band had a special domain over which it held sway and in which it even exercised functions of public security, in the sense that, having the monopoly of criminal action and of the resultant spoils, it took energetic measures in its own interests to check the activity of any other malefactors. In fact, even as late as 1926, the chief of the band of the Madonie was called *"u prefetto"* and the *latitante* Sacco di Raffaldi was called *"u maresciallo."* It happened sometimes that when an armed band showed a tendency to extend its domain too far, other *latitanti* and bandits united into a new band to oppose it, or it even happened that, owing to the complete absence or failure of the police, a few landowners whose livelihood and property were threatened by excessive extortion and *taglie* on the part of an armed band, had to hire other criminals for their own defence, and these ended in forming a new band. It is needless to say that, if these bands of various origin sometimes had fierce battles with one another, they sometimes ended by coming to terms, to the detriment of the rural population and the landowners.

As the armed bands died out, the *gruppo armato* (armed group) grew up in the country districts, but it was of quite an ephemeral character, often only occasional, being almost always a mixture of *latitanti* and free criminals, transitory in its influence and sporadic in action. The armed band was a *state* of criminal existence which produced a particular state of things in its district: the armed group was simply a criminal *gesture* which left but a momentary trace on its district. The group only opposed to the action of the authorities the surmountable obstacle presented by the number of its components: but the band opposed the very serious obstacle of compulsory *omertà* and obligatory assistance which were implicit in the depressed state of mind they created round them.

In fighting an armed group one had men of flesh and blood and muskets in front of one. So that victory was only a question of will. In the fight against an armed band one had in front of one, before one came to men and muskets, an elusive, undefinable, but infectious state of local feeling which cut one off from men's hearts, shut men's mouths and slackened even the bravest man's grip of his weapon. It was fear: not instinctive physical fear, but fear born of just anxiety for a man's family and his possessions, or of the far from unlikely prospect of his child being kidnapped, his brother killed, his wife having a miscarriage from fright, his daughter being raped, hundreds of animals stolen, or his farm being set on fire, as a reprisal for trying to free himself from the infamous yoke, especially if he asked the constituted authorities for protection.

As I have said, the armed bands died out. But the *solitary* criminals were numerous—*latitanti* or bandits of high class, whose very class made them despise others, unless they commanded them, and prefer to keep to themselves. The bandits of this kind preferred to keep to themselves for a rather prosaic reason, but a utilitarian one, which is expressed in the common proverb: *meglio soli che male accompagnati* (better alone than with bad companions). Like the armed band, the solitary bandit, either by intimidation or by the aid of a relic of that unhealthy sympathy with which the ingenuous rural mind surrounded fugitives from justice when justice was not really just, creates round himself an atmosphere of favour and even of complicity which protects him. Of this he regularly takes advantage but it also renders him liable to a subtle form of blackmail since, by his very solitariness, his life and liberty are at the mercy of those who favour him. In fact, spy-mania is a characteristic of the solitary bandit: the spy is the only enemy of whom he is continuously afraid. On this point he is inexorable: a doubtful attitude, a word, a suspicion, are enough for him to kill without pity. The solitary bandit, also, has his particular sphere of influence, in which he behaves exactly like the armed bands, with the same effects and results, i.e. local anxiety, a monopoly of criminal activity, blackmail, interference with other people's affairs, *taglie* and, in exchange, a defence of public security by the violent elimination of other malefactors. On this last head the solitary bandit has a special reason for interfering, since not a few criminals allow themselves to operate in his name, or deliberately supplant him, especially in signing blackmailing letters. He wages savage warfare on these, executing summary justice according to his custom.

Some years ago at M., a widow landowner without relations was robbed in the first instance of forty oxen which she could only recover by paying a large sum to the local Mafia. According to the rules she ought to have been left in peace after that. Instead, after a little time, the same animals were stolen again. Again she paid ransom for them. A few months later they were stolen a third time. Evidently the malefactors were taking undue advantage of her being a lonely widow. At this point, however, she went to see a very redoubtable bandit who held sway in the district and asked him for justice, offering him money. "There is no need of that," he said, and refused the money. A week later, having found out that the men responsible for the triple theft were two prosperous *mafiosi* of another village, he shot them both while they were driving in a trap to an appointment that he made with them on some other pretext.

Such were the relations of the *latitanti* and bandits with the population: so far as the police are concerned, even when numerous and well armed, they prefer to avoid contact with it, nor are they prone to lay in ambush for it. Nevertheless they will take up arms and fight bravely when they have been surprised and find themselves with their backs to the wall. The fights which then occur between *latitanti* and the police not seldom have tragic consequences. It is curious to note in this connection, that up to the other day—for it no longer holds good under the Fascist régime—in such conflicts the first shot had to be fired by the bandits. Arms were given to the police simply for self-defence, not in order to assert the sovereignty of the law against all who wished to escape from it by armed force, so that, in order to make legal use of arms against *latitanti* armed and determined to resist, the police were required to wait until they were placed by their opponents in the position of legitimate self-defence, that is, in a definitely inferior position. If, as a result of this, a police agent fell at the first shot or a bandit succeeded in escaping, there was always the consolation that the law had not been broken. However, this was never the real difficulty; for nobody splits legal hairs with a gun in his hand.

A far more serious hindrance than was supposed was the difficulty of recognising the *latitanti*, which might sometimes lead to dangerous perplexity. This was principally due to the fact that, as soon as a criminal went into hiding, all his photographs disappeared from his home and copies could not be obtained for distribution.

But the real difficulty of hunting down the *latitante* is of a physiological nature. The *latitante* has over the police agent the advantage of being able to reduce his physical needs to a minimum without harm. The bandits and their horses can live, if need be, and march for whole days and nights on end without food, without drink, without sleep, without speaking, without quinine, or castor oil, or iodine, or soap, or combs, or boots or horse-shoes. I know that by personal experience. And I know it so well that, when I had to take personal charge of a man-hunt, I used to put the armed force placed at my disposal through a strict course of physical training so as to turn them, as the phrase goes, into *uomini di legno e cavalli di ferro* (men of wood and horses of iron). To this, as well as to the dash and courage of my men, I owe the fact that, when I gained immediate contact with them, I always got the better of the *latitanti* and bandits I was hunting.

They were long and arduous pursuits, full of sacrifice and discomfort, for which, when I came down from the lurking dangers of the hills and forests, my consolation was to see the ploughs quietly at work, the flocks safely wandering in the pastures, the long, jingling lines of loaded waggons passing unmolested along the roads. And I found a special satisfaction in the expressions of humble folk who sometimes showed their feelings in unstudied words. While I was exercising my functions there was held at Palermo a certain agricultural gathering in which some real peasants took part. And among these was an old fellow who, at the end of the meeting, having pushed his way up to me, said with a voice that thrilled with suppressed feeling: *"Eccellenza: erano dieci anni c'a mi scecca 'un vidia i stidde!"* (Your Excellency, my mule hadn't seen the stars for ten years!) He meant that at last, after ten years of having to keep her shut up during the hours of darkness lest she should be stolen, he was able to go about at night with his mule. And he was right, because cattle-raiding had reached such a pitch that the peasants preferred to leave their animals in the village and go to their work on foot, even to long distances, or, if they had to use animals for their work, to leave the village in broad daylight and come back before sunset. And this led to a noticeable shortening of the working hours with a corresponding loss of production and injury to the economic state of the island.

# My Earlier Battles With Bandits

I have been engaged in chasing *latitanti* since my earliest years, and I could tell many stories of the chase. But I will only tell two which are characteristic because of their attendant circumstances.

In May, 1916, I was ordered to go to Sicily from which I had been absent for a year, in order to assist in a special service which was being organised with the aim of remedying the deplorable state of public safety in the four western provinces of the island. These had been very sorely tried by the intense activity of numerous criminals and, in particular, by the audacity of two armed bands: one of these, the Carlino band, working on foot, consisting of three young *latitanti* who had been joined by some free criminals, had been for many months troubling the southern part of the province of Caltanissetta, with their centre at Riesi; and the other, the Grisafi band, working on horseback, consisting of five regular bandits who were often joined by other *latitanti*, had been for years plaguing the western part of the province of Agrigento and the neighbouring districts of the provinces of Palermo and Trapani, with its centre at Caltabellotta. When I reached Palermo, I was given direction of the police services in the provinces of Caltanissetta and Agrigento, so that the chase of both bands fell within my competence.

After staying some days at Palermo to organise my personnel, I went to Caltanissetta, where everything, both people and country, was new to me. I set to work by concentrating particularly on the Carlino band, round which terror had created a quite impenetrable veil of mystery and some rather baseless legends. A few months before there had been added to the various murders committed by the band, that of a brave *carabiniere* who, surprised by the bandits at daybreak while he was going from Riesi to the distant railway station to spend a few days' leave in his own village, had fallen after a gallant fight with muskets. After this tragic episode, the police had redoubled their energies, combing out the country by general drives in force or by special operations, guided by the rare and vague information which they sometimes managed to procure—information that was always inconclusive in spite of the large price that the Government had put on the leader's head.

All this, however, though it undoubtedly showed courage and determination on the part of the police, only produced the very same inconvenient state of things that had led to so many failures: it troubled the waters, and so assisted the hunted men. The system of congesting the countryside with armed men and of keeping them continually on the move is not the best adapted for hunting down *latitanti*. On the most favourable hypothesis it can only result in driving the quarry outside the district that is being searched. It is wrong to suppose that by multiplying the number of movements of the police one increases the probabilities of a chance meeting with the *latitanti*. In reality, exactly the opposite occurs: the greater the force and the more it moves about, the easier it is to see and, therefore, the less likelihood it has of lighting on the quarry. The battle with the *latitanti* is rather like that of love: *vince che fugge*, or he who can keep out of the way wins. That sounds a paradox, but it is true. To know how to keep out of the way is, in this field, the best way of being there at the right moment: to know how to remain inactive is the best way of being able to act when action is necessary. Eight days' inactivity for an hour's action; a month's absence for five minutes on the spot: that is the way to do it. One prepares for a bandit-hunt by letting the local sediment settle; it is carried on by stealth and concluded by surprise.

When one has made up one's mind to act in earnest, the neighbourhood should be left absolutely quiet. Only thus can it be clearly scrutinised and all the psychological and material data be collected which it is necessary to know for the direction and development of the action. From a hundred to three hundred men on foot or on horseback moving about the district make this difficult: a few men are enough, and one alone is best, with his head screwed on the right way, his heart in the right place and his nerves of steel. Two ends are attained in this way: the bandits, not being disturbed, not only stay where they are but are lulled into security and allow their movements to be more easily seen; and the structure and nature of the protective system that aids them is revealed. This is of capital importance, since according to the character, quality, behaviour and family position of the bandits, the reasons for their *latitanza* and their subsequent interference in all kinds of local activities and interests, the difficulties created by the protective system that surrounds them vary in kind. They may be of a passive kind, born simply of fear, or of an active nature inspired by a hundred considerations, not excluding sentimental or even—formerly—electoral ones. It is clear that, once all these factors have been observed and closely scrutinised, the subsequent action, of stealth and surprise, will at least be based on rational lines.

To come back to the particular instance I am speaking of, a few days after my arrival, I learnt that Carlino and Co. were taking advantage of the frequent absences of the police on their usual operations in the country to come into the village at night and stay there roystering with women of ill-repute. I paid special regard to this, as it seemed to me to correspond perfectly with the unbridled, dissolute character and the youth of the bandits. About three weeks passed, and then one of the usual pieces of information came in. The band had been seen going about in full war-paint on a steep mountain that rises about 15 kilometres from Riesi. I did not believe it. I was gradually coming to the conclusion that the former reports of that kind, which had regularly been followed by unsuccessful operations, were of doubtful origin, that is, that they were put about by friends of the bandits to entice the police away from certain points and concentrate them in other places where there was nothing to find.

Something told me that this fresh piece of information, which had come in an apparently urgent and circumstantial form, was of that kind, and had the same origin, perhaps with the aim of testing the probable direction in which I, the new commander, should take action. There was nothing to prove this: it was only an inner voice that came from some twist of my sub-conscious mind—a voice that has spoken to me more than once, and to which I have always listened. Perhaps what is called *good luck* is simply due to this inner voice, in so far as sudden intuitions sometimes lead to unexpected successes, though involving the illogical dismissal of more carefully thought-out plans. However, that may be, I listened to it again. And what followed was typical of its results.

I need not say that as soon as this new information was received, I was warmly recommended to undertake one of the usual operations—a sudden concentration of force by night to surround the foot of the incriminated mountain completely, and a subsequent enveloping movement by pushing the whole force up the slopes to the top of the mountain. If the bandits were there, as had been reported, they would be unable to escape. It was mathematically certain: but—were they there? I asked that question, and I was answered on all sides that they certainly were. "There is too much certainty," I thought: "so the bandits are somewhere else." So I enthusiastically agreed to the proposed operation, and gave orders that almost the whole of the armed force of which I disposed should take part in it. It would take four days to carry out.

Meanwhile, on my own account, on the afternoon of the third day, when the heat of the mountain would be just at its height, I got on my horse and left Caltanissetta unobserved with three men by the lonely road that leads through the open country to Riesi. As I reached the neighbourhood of Riesi it was getting dark. A long and dense procession of peasants, almost all mounted on horses, mules or donkeys, and waggons of every kind was pouring, as it did every evening, from the fields to the village in a dense cloud of dust, through which, in the growing dusk, men and animals took on indistinct and nebulous shapes. The peasants, their eyes swollen with the sun, dust, fatigue and sleep, went along in a dull and dreamy silence. My men and I scattered and worked our way into the long column; I adapted myself to its lounging pace, its sleepy appearance and its dumbness, and, under convenient cloak of dust, horse-flies and the reek of horses, I got into the village quite unobserved, though I had never been there before and did not know one stone of it from another. When it reached the houses, the long column split up as each man went his way into the lanes. I followed one lane at a venture, and caught a glimpse of the police station. Naturally I went past it, and, cautiously followed by my three men, I halted at a lonely and deserted corner from which, favoured by the darkness which the few street lamps did not make less thick, I went quietly and alone, like one of the inhabitants, to the police station: and my men joined me there a little later, they having been able to stable their horses in the barracks without arousing suspicion in the general confusion of the returning peasants.

My main object was therefore attained, since the chief thing was to get into the heart of the position unobserved. Half an hour had not gone by when news came to the office where I was, that the *latitanti* Tofalo and Carlino had come into the village a short time ago mingled with the same column of peasants in which I had come in, that is to say from the direction immediately opposite to that of the mountain which at that moment was occupied by the police force. It was quite obvious: profiting by the absence of the armed force which had been attracted away by false information, the *latitanti* had come to the village to make a night of it undisturbed. But where? In such places, it is true, the women of ill-repute are so few and so notorious that they are all known and may be counted on the fingers. Thus, the women with whom the bandits usually went were known, but nobody in the police could tell me where they assembled. And Riesi is not so small a place that one can find one's way about it easily without knowing it, especially at night. Meanwhile, so as not to give the alarm, it was absolutely indispensable that the whole of the police (twenty-five men) who were present in the village, with their leaders and officers, should remain still and indoors. Towards midnight, the streets being deserted and silent, I decided to act.

A police official had been able to find out that the two low women who were friends of the bandits were absent from their houses. That confirmed the idea that the bandits were in the village with them. By a process of exclusions and inductions founded on a few timid words murmured by people living near, I was able at last to locate the place where the meetings were probably held and, after a quick and silent inspection, the block of buildings in which the meeting-place must be. It was a block made of a long row of hovels, consolidated into a single construction, in the heart of a populous quarter; and not even the police agents of the place knew its internal plan, its arrangement and the ways of possible communication between the hovels. It was no use losing time in conjecture or plans of operation: the thing was to find out if the bandits were there and to act at once.

With a part of the force I surrounded the whole block on the outside: with the rest I went up to the first house in the row and demanded admission. The door was opened without hesitation. There was nobody there except the small family of peasants who lived there. While the police officials and men were finishing the inspection of the premises and asking a few questions, I went out into the street. I was slightly disappointed, and I leant against the rather rickety door of the hovel next door to the one I had left, and exchanged a few words with one of the officials. Suddenly, as I was speaking, I distinctly heard behind the door against which I was leaning the stamp of an animal's hoof. At that time and in such a place animals were never left alone. Where an animal was shut up somebody else was sure to be shut up too. After having knocked at the door repeatedly without effect, I called: "Open the door!"

Dead silence. I was now sure I was right. "Open the door," I repeated, "or I'll have it broken in."

A silence of the grave. Turning to some of the police agents who had come out of the house and were standing round, I said: "Break in that door."

Hardly had I uttered the words than two musket shots were fired from behind the very door. The bullets slapped against the wall opposite without hurting anybody. This visiting card left no doubts and demanded an immediate and adequate reply. My men, dashing to one side and lying down, returned the fire and the battle opened very furiously. When the first fury had spent itself, I made sure that the blockade round the block of houses was such as to prevent all flight or surprise on the part of the bandits, and I took every possible means to give the greatest possible effect to our own fire. In my ignorance of the number of the *latitanti* that I had to deal with, and also of the internal arrangements of the place they were in, and in the impossibility of picking out a target behind that door which, rickety and weak as it was, though it allowed a free passage to the bullets of both sides, gave the bandits a certain view of their target while it completely hid ours—I decided to maintain my assault at the highest intensity so as to clear up the situation as quickly as possible. So there, in the darkness of the night, in the radius of a few yards, a desperate and deadly battle went on between unknown adversaries firing blind and sudden volleys. Although our fire was rather oblique and low owing to the narrowness of the street, and though my men (being completely exposed) had to fire prone, the old door was gradually splintering to bits, so that I saw the moment approaching for a sudden rush that should carry the door, the bandits and everything with them. The bandits, however, in spite of the fire of three of my men which was sweeping the door and its surroundings from loopholes made, after the first exchanges, in the wall of the house opposite, had obviously found a position out of range of our fire; they kept up wild and intermittent firing from the now enlarged cracks in the door, showing how alert and well provided with ammunition they were. The village, awakened by the noise of the firing, kept within doors, in silence and in darkness. But it was summer, and dawn was quickly approaching. At the first streak, as soon as it was light enough for me to see the position, I descried an opening at the back of the block which led to a little staircase giving access to a room above that in which the bandits were. I immediately occupied it and had the floor pierced with an iron bar, thus making a loophole in it in spite of the shots which the *latitanti*, guessing my intention, concentrated on the hole from below. The position of the bandits was now tragic. Under fire from the front, from the flank and from above, and reduced to taking cover beneath a flight of stairs from which they could not possibly fire except for honour's sake, they lost heart and, as they afterwards confessed, thought of surrendering, but could not make up their minds to do so for fear of losing their lives. I was now determined to carry the place with a rush.

Just at that moment Carlino's mother and an uncle of his, who were certainly aware of the dangerous position the bandits were in, came to me and asked if they might make an attempt to induce Carlino and his companions to surrender before the fight ended in inevitable tragedy. I thought I could not reject the mother's request, so I gave her five minutes in which to make the attempt. I ordered a cease-fire, and shouted to the *latitanti* that if they did not surrender in five minutes, I would resume firing till they were all killed. Then Carlo's mother, taking cover behind the angle of the house, called *"Figghiu!"* (son), and Carlino replied with an equally loud cry *"Matre!"* Some brief motherly exhortations followed, till the bandits shouted that they surrendered and asked for their lives to be spared. I answered that they must throw down their arms and come out into the open. They obeyed immediately.

They were the *latitanti*, Carlino and Tofalo, with two free criminals as their companions. Two loose women were with them. They were armed with Mauser muskets, automatic pistols of the most modern kind, long clasp-knives and sword-bayonets, besides having field-glasses. They had fired about three hundred rounds between them, and still had two hundred rounds in reserve. Carlino and Tofalo confessed that, with another bandit who had left them a few days before, they had murdered the *carabiniere* I mentioned above, besides committing another fourfold murder, an act of attempted homicide which failed, and about twenty offences of blackmail. Their two companions swore they were as innocent as doves.

Having cleared matters up in the province of Caltanissetta, I went on to that of Agrigento, where the state of things was rather different. The *latitante*, Grisafi, a mountain-dweller of thirty-six years of age, originally a shepherd, who commanded the armed band there, was a consummate bandit. Fierce and cautious, most redoubtable, up to all the tricks and stratagems of guerrilla warfare, and protected by a thick net of local favour strengthened by terror, he had been a *latitante* for quite twelve years; and he had set up in the western part of the province a kind of special domain over which he ruled absolutely, interfering in every kind of affair, even the most intimate, making his will felt in every field, including the electoral field, and levying tolls and taxes, blackmailing and committing crimes of bloodshed without stint. Some thirty murders were put down to him, besides an unending series of crimes. Perhaps he had not committed so many: possibly he had committed more: certainly he was ready to go on committing them. They called him *Marcuzzo* (little Mark), but he was a man of thews and muscles, inclined to stoutness.

Aided not only by his boldness but by constant good luck, and being a good shot, he had always succeeded in escaping from the toils of the police; he had escaped unhurt from several conflicts and had sometimes inflicted loss on his pursuers. Not long after I came to the province of Agrigento, during a raid on the southern part of the province of Palermo, he had run into a group of five police agents with his whole band. Instead of opening fire, as was his wont, he had beaten a hasty retreat over the gentle slope of a small hill, disappearing from view over its shoulder. The police agents had immediately rushed in pursuit, but in their zeal they had not thought of the trap laid for them. Instead of coming on in open order, they had kept close together. Grisafi and his companions were waiting for them on the other side of the slope: and a well-aimed volley caught the pursuers full at their first appearance on the skyline, killing two brave men. For some time, too, Grisafi had had such a reputation for being uncapturable that the country folk began seriously to believe that he was *maato* (bewitched). The thing was ridiculous, as well as being very regrettable, and it had to be put an end to at once, not only for reasons of duty, but also for those of prestige.

I took on the job, and, with a small party of young and brave officials, including a *carabiniere* officer, I pitched some tents on a beach at Sciacca, a charming and hospitable little town, in whose rocky hinterland there rise, about twenty kilometres away, three typical rocky peaks, immediately overhanging the picturesque village of Caltabellotta, Grisafi's native place. According to my system, I told my assistants that the probabilities of success would be in direct proportion to the tangible proofs we could give of inactivity, indolence and ineptitude. It was my idea, in fact, that as soon as we succeeded in being regarded as a useless party of more or less stupid idlers, we should have a nine to one chance of success.

After the end of Carlino and Co., my arrival in the province of Agrigento had aroused some anxiety. I was told that, a few days after my arrival, the Grisafi band, which apparently numbered nine men at that time, had been reduced to six. Three of the bandits had preferred to go off on their own affairs. After a little time had elapsed another bandit had gone away, owing to some dispute with the leader, and the band had been reduced to five—Grisafi, his brother, the two brothers Maniscalco and a certain Santangelo. At that rate there was the risk that the famous band would disappear into thin air, and I wanted to capture it, not to break it up. By capturing it entire, I cut the evil at the root: by forcing it to disband I accomplished nothing; or worse, I simply dissolved the evil in the neighbourhood. It was necessary, therefore, to reassure them as to my intentions by some thoroughly stupid action.

Sciacca, among other things, is famous for its hot springs, for its mullet and its soles. So I and some of my subordinates suddenly found ourselves affected with rheumatic pains and took a strict course of treatment for them—morning baths, reaction, lunch off mullet, afternoon sleep, digestive promenade, dinner off soles, a game of cards, another little walk and so to bed. We did it all openly, in the local hotel, with revolting persistence and entire want of shame. Every now and again we took an innocent little ride in the neighbourhood, and that was all.

Nobody, of course, knew that by night, in our little rooms that were tightly closed against all intrusions, the work of study and preparation was busily going on. And people began to ask if we had come to Sciacca to take the water-cure or to catch the Grisafi band. I was really glad when I heard this. Meanwhile the police force at my disposal remained concentrated at certain places specially selected, so that, while apparently scattered and distant, it was really in complete readiness and quite handy. The Grisafi band, which had eyes everywhere, became reassured and remained quietly on the look out, awaiting events, in the district between Sciacca and Caltabellotta.

It was then that I began to send out my men, cautiously, one by one, without any preparation and on the most bureaucratic excuses, into the various places that had been the scenes of the bandits' crimes, in order to collect—without raising the alarm and so without any official formality—all possible current news on the past activities of the band and especially the necessary indications for indentifying their habitual and occasional helpers, whether voluntary accomplices or compelled by fear. There was need for haste because, if the game went on too long, it would be found out. Their work was carried out quickly and quietly with as good results as could possibly be obtained in such conditions: and feverish activity, all night long, reigned in the little bedrooms of the Sciacca hotel.

Now, if in the province of Caltanissetta a certain number of helpers bound simply by terror or bonds of complicity had grown up round the Carlino band, insufficient to hinder seriously the action of the authorities, the network of assistance that had been drawn round the Grisafi band had grown wide, thick and strong in the course of time. The whole system was welded together by complicity in crimes, fear of reprisals, terror, espionage on behalf of the bandits, conflicting interests and equivocal alliances for the most varied ends, to an extent that made it almost impenetrable. To attempt victory by trying to circumvent it would have been an arduous task, and would in any case have created a danger in our rear. If we wanted to get at the band, we had to confront it, annihilate and finish it off at a blow, all in one piece and with all its ramifications. We had to arrest simultaneously all Grisafi's helpers and keep them under arrest till the bandits were caught.

The idea in itself had not the attraction of novelty; for over and over again attempts to capture *latitanti* had been marked by the arrest more or less *en masse* of their helpers; but just because it had been abused, the manoeuvre, against which high-class *latitanti* always took precautions, had become particularly difficult. And in this case, through a complication of special circumstances, the difficulties of the operation were immense. But it would undoubtedly dismay and confuse the bandits, if such an assertion of will and power occurred after so many years of inaction, and would at the same time draw the neighbourhood to our side owing to the immediate rise in the prestige of the State. In its concrete effects it would isolate the bandits in a more or less neutral environment which would allow us to get direct contact with them, and mean their certain capture. But it would be necessary to gain complete and accurately timed success: even a partial failure would be disastrous. And there was no time to be lost.

One night, therefore, by sudden simultaneous action in different places, I made an attempt to arrest all the helpers we had identified and against whom—at my own request, which had been kept secret—the judicial authorities had issued warrants of arrest: 357 persons in all, of whom ninety were in Caltabellotta alone. The attempt succeeded perfectly and without incident. But there was one amusing thing. The officials found in the possession of Grisafi's old father, who was among the arrested persons, some scrip of a national loan that was being subscribed at the time, an obvious fruit of his son's labours. When asked to explain how he got it, the old man with a quiet and patriotic smile answered that he too had done what he could for his country. This extensive and unexpected action, not least on account of the standing of some of the arrested persons, made a profound impression and produced the effects that I had foreseen. There was only one thing that I feared, namely, that the band would be dissolved in view of the turn affairs had taken.

But this did not happen. On the dawn of the third day after the arrests, a large black flag, fixed to a mast on the highest of the three peaks overlooking Caltabellotta, appeared fluttering in the keen mountain breeze. In this way the band asserted its presence and its intentions. And now, our mutual positions being unmasked, the fight became openly declared, close and uninterrupted.

I have already said that one bandit, owing to a dispute with Grisafi, had left him a little while after my arrival in the province of Agrigento. There were some indications of his presence in a district adjacent to that held by the band to whom, perhaps, he thought of giving the benefit of his assistance. A brave police official undertook to deal with him, and one night, with a party of police and *carabinieri*, he succeeded in surprising and surrounding him. A violent conflict ensued. The bandit finally surrendered, but one gallant soldier was killed and the official, seriously wounded in the chest, had to be taken hurriedly to the local *carabinieri* barracks. The populace, who had begun to take heart after the arrests, became a little depressed. I immediately intervened, and over the bloodstained remains of the poor *carabiniere* who had heroically fallen in the name of duty I made a solemn, public declaration that the end of the famous band was decided, sure and close at hand. The Mafia took care to answer on the band's behalf.

A few days after the *carabiniere's* funeral, a criminal of the neighbourhood died of natural causes in prison, and the Mafia arranged to make his funeral the occasion of an imposing demonstration, summoning all its members from all the villages of the district to the function. The funeral procession with its brass bands was to march through the principal street of the place, pass in front of the barracks of the *carabinieri* and under the windows of the very room where the wounded official was still lying and halt at the cemetery where was the still fresh grave of the poor *carabiniere*. Although it was secretly prepared, the plan leaked out and came to my knowledge, so I took up my position on the main street, which I had patrolled. At a given moment the hearse arrived at the entrance to the village. After a short halt to form the procession, as had been arranged, the funeral *cortège* advanced along its prearranged route. At the sides of the road, and in front of the houses and shops, little groups of curious observers, especially countrywomen and girls, were standing waiting. I too stood waiting, till the procession reached the place where I was standing. First came the priest, then the hearse, then the group of relations and intimate friends. I made no movement. But when I saw, a few paces behind this group, a band playing a raucous dirge and a dense body of people who wanted to make the funeral an excuse for making a demonstration of their presence and their intimidating power, which was an insult, I came forward and stopped them. Two words were enough: "Go away!" and a point of the hand to the direction they had come from. Perhaps my voice roused some obscure echo in their consciences, for they turned about like one man and went off in a twinkling with their band.

In the other direction the hearse, preceded by the holy symbols of the Christian faith, and followed by the group of mourners, went on slowly and silently to its destination in the sad majesty of death which levels all, the bad and the good, before human pity and Divine mercy. I went off to the barracks. As I went by, there arose from the groups of women and girls who had been waiting to see the funeral a murmur of brief phrases: *ci vulia* (that's what was wanted), *un se ne putia cchiù!* (it was too much to put up with!) *bbono!* (good!) and *binirittu!* (bless you!) That was enough for me. It is needless to say that, like the arrest *en masse* of the helpers, the episode of the funeral had some repercussions both near and far, with some due exaggeration and apposite comment. But I had been too long accustomed to such repercussions and comments to pay much attention to them.

We were now really at close quarters. The Grisafi band preferred to remain on the heights where it undoubtedly had a place of refuge. I attempted a sudden enveloping movement, and the band was caught in it. Grisafi himself, after his capture, confessed this to me, and he added that more than once on that day he had us within range from the peak on which the band was posted, but that he had not fired—very kind of him!—so as not to attract in his direction all the parties of police by which he saw himself surrounded. However, during the night, the bandits got away by impenetrable tracks only known to themselves. But we at last found their base refuge: a cave high up in the hills which one reached through a hole in the rock that could not be singled out at a distance. Beyond the hole which formed its entrance, the cave broadened out into a large space, fitted as a stable for horses and provided with a fine manger of cement. Beyond the stable the cave gradually narrowed, funnel-wise, for a sufficient length to provide sleeping places for the men, and it ended in a kind of chimney in which had been cut rough steps, which came out in the open across a small and unsuspected rocky pinnacle. The effect of this discovery was at once apparent. Two days later five horses were found abandoned and wandering about in the country round Sciacca. These horses belonged to the bandits, for whom their mounts had now become an embarrassment. Naturally I pretended to have understood nothing and to believe that it was a case of cattle-stealing. I protested loudly at the audacity of cattle-thieves and I sent out circular telegrams to find out where the theft had taken place. On the other hand, during the two nights following, I had each of the horses mounted in turn by a police agent and left free to go where it would, so that from the direction that the animal invariably took I was able to draw precious conclusions as to the direction in which the police should move. It was the moment to come to grips.

The Grisafi band, now on foot and without support, moved very little and, owing to the fewness of the houses where it could take refuge, had necessarily to go round the caves. From certain vague information, moreover, I knew that it was keeping near the town with the strange intention of making a nocturnal incursion and giving us a "serenade" under the windows of our quiet hotel. One day, late in the afternoon, I learnt with comparative certainty that the band would be found that same night in a certain cave looking on the sea, a few kilometers from Sciacca. The indications as to the exact topographical position of the cave were rather vague, but there was no time to make sure of them. It was obviously a perfect night for the enterprise: it was the middle of January and the weather was beastly.

That night, the police officials and men having assembled, I left for the place in question, guided by an old police agent belonging to the place, whom I had suddenly called in at the last moment. When we came to the neighbourhood of the cave, we found that it was a kind of huge platform from the edge of which steep and rocky slopes led down to the sea, and the bandits' cave opened off one of these. It was pitch dark, there was a hurricane of wind and the rain came down in torrents. I halted the party on the high ground and, accompanied by one or two officers and the old guide, I began to go down a kind of footpath to reconnoitre the place and the way to it, my companions muttering low curses against the band at every fresh squall of rain. At a certain point our path, which went straight down to the sea, crossed another that ran parallel to the beach. According to the indications I had we ought to have gone to the right: but our old guide—who had not yet been told the object of our expedition, but had evidently guessed it—said the path stopped to the right, and that we must turn to the left. I was not convinced, but he stuck to his opinion. A short turn in both directions did not clear up the doubt; and a false move might have alarmed the band and sent it flying heaven knows where. It was still the dead of night and we had not been seen by anyone. So I went back to the high ground, collected all my men and went cautiously back to the town, where I sent them all to bed, though I kept the old guide under lock and key so that he should not come into contact with anybody.

Next night I repeated the attempt, I blockaded the position according to my own principles and advanced at dawn. I had been right. The old guide had not been deceitful, but he only knew the place from hazy recollections of his far-off youth. The cave was found: a real fortress very well furnished with provisions. But the bandits were not there. There were fresh traces of them, namely, a strip of paper hung on the wall with dabs of shaving soap on it. Evidently the band had gone out on some expedition, and now that we had arrived would not come back to that place. But it would be within range. So I went back to the town and openly moved some of my men to places some way off so that the band should not go away.

Two days passed: and on the morning of the third day I heard that by night I should get information of the band's new place of refuge. I said nothing to any one, so that the expression of ill-concealed commiseration at our recent disappointment should stay on everybody's face; but I had a strong party of police sent cautiously down towards the town from a village nearby and concealed it a few hundred yards from the houses in a tunnel of a branch railway line then being constructed. By evening I knew that the band was in a country cottage about eight hundred yards as the crow flies from the town, on the opposite lip of a deep valley that runs to the west of the town and immediately below it. But the indications were not enough to ensure the certain success of a surprise, which was also made very difficult because our advance on the cottage would inevitably rouse all the watch-dogs in the numerous habitations which were scattered all over the small tract we should have to pass through. I still said nothing. We had dinner as usual; we played our usual game of cards and had our little walk; then we went to bed. Only then did I tell them all to stay in their rooms, in the dark, dressed and in readiness.

As for me, having somewhat disguised myself, I went out unobserved a little later, and in a short time got further indications as to the position of the cottage, its configuration and the way to it. Of its internal arrangement I learnt nothing. One useful thing I found out was that the cottage had a rustic courtyard in front of it surrounded by a high wall with a big, strong door. At the back it had a balcony looking on the town and particularly favourable for the bandits' fire. I went back to the hotel, and a little after midnight I assembled all my men under the tunnel, where the force remained waiting for an hour or two.

To discount the inevitable alarm that would be given by all the dogs it was necessary that the encirclement of the cottage should take place in dead silence, with the utmost rapidity and with mathematical precision. But nobody knew its position, and in the thick darkness that wrapped the countryside it was extremely difficult to find one's way. I formed four squads, commanded by excellent police officers and two officers of the *carabinieri* who were voluntarily joined by a young cavalry lieutenant who was doing police duty in the district; and I assigned them the task of surrounding the cottage at not more than thirty yards' distance, allotting to each squad the side of the cottage it was to face.

The orders were to march quickly and silently, to reach all positions simultaneously, each squad to extend opposite the side of the house allotted to it, immediate communication to be established between all so that there should be no gaps, especially between one squad and the next, and to wait without moving from their posts on any pretext whatever. If anybody came out of the cottage, they were to fire but not move. If they were fired at from the cottage, they were to reply but not move. I said I would give final orders on the spot according to circumstances. Having assigned a particular route to each squad, so that all should reach their positions on the four sides simultaneously, I sent them off at short successive intervals, according to the distance they each had to travel. When the last squad had moved off I also went towards the place. It was a short march; it was a very dark night, as I have said: so that everything should have been favourable to surprise.

Suddenly, however, dogs began loudly barking in front of us, and the barking spread to our flanks and accompanied our footsteps. The men ducked their heads as though under a shower of hail and, muttering low curses against the friend of man, quickened their pace. I was highly annoyed, the famous cottage being too near for the bandits not to have heard the dreadful noise. Nevertheless, I did not lose heart. A few minutes later the squads were at their posts, extended in an unbroken line round the cottage. My men found some cover behind clumps of cactus, trees or bits of tumbledown wall, but most of them lay in the open. The squad in front of the balcony was entirely without cover. It was half past two in the morning when our wait began.

Many minutes had not gone by when the big door of the yard was opened cautiously to let a man out. The squad in front opened fire, just one round. The door shut with a bang, and the man who came out disappeared into the darkness. A few moments later a sudden volley was fired from the balcony at the back. The squad below it replied and there followed a rapid exchange of heavy fire. The band evidently wanted to test the position. So, to scatter any illusions or hopes on their part, I shouted to the force: "Fire from all sides!" when I could make myself heard. A heavy discharge struck the cottage on every side: the bandits now knew what they were up against.

A long pause followed on both sides. I had no interest in continuing to fire while the thick darkness still prevented our even seeing the windows. It was enough to hold on to the position. At daybreak I should have light to see my way. The bandits, however, did not take the same view. Being under cover, they began firing again with the evident intention of provoking reply from us, so that they could accurately single out our positions one by one. With this end in view they pushed some rolled-up mattresses out on to the balcony so that, standing behind them, they could bring their fire further forward. The fight went on in this way, with shots on both sides rather wildly aimed in the dark and with sudden volleys till dawn.

At the first streak of dawn the *latitanti* ceased fire. They were obviously having a council of war. I took advantage of this to inspect my men and give each of them orders for the decisive action: but I was seen, and fire was opened again. I was moving along the posts in front of the yard door when, in the thick of a clump of cactus near the wall of the yard, I saw the outline of two boot-soles. On my order two agents seized them and pulled vigorously. It was a man—the one who had come out of the door in the night shortly after our arrival. He was a peasant, the tenant of the surrounded cottage in which he lived with his wife. Half dead with fear, he told us that three days before Grisafi and his complete band had suddenly turned up and ordered him with dire threats of death to give him and his men food and lodging. He had had to obey and had been even compelled to go down to the town several times on errands for the bandits, while his wife was kept as a hostage. The afternoon of the preceding day he had been told to go to the town to see what I was doing. He had come, had watched me, and when he had seen me go quietly back to the hotel with my officers and go to bed, he had come back to the cottage to say that all was quiet in the town and that I was snoring hard.

This had so reassured the bandits that, while keeping their clothes on, they laid themselves down to sleep the sleep of the just. The barking of the dogs had awakened them, but had not roused their suspicion; the first suspicions had come from the noise my men had made in surrounding the house. One of them, the poor man added, had said it was probably only some animals got loose; but Grisafi, collecting the whole band with muskets loaded, had gone down, placed himself behind the door of the yard and told him to go out and see what was up. So he had had to go out. Greeted by our first volley, the poor fellow had been forced to take a lightning decision between two courses—either to go back into the yard with the probability of being killed by the bandits on the suspicion of treachery or to go on with the probability of being killed by the police on a contrary suspicion. "In my awful doubt," he said, "I had a sudden inspiration: to pretend to be killed. I threw myself motionless on the ground in the clump of cactus from which you have just dragged me."

We heard afterwards from the bandits themselves that, after the volley that had greeted the owner's exit, they had pretended to shut the door, but had remained behind it in the hope we would rush in. When this hope failed, they had shut and bolted the door and had gone out on to the balcony and opened fire from it to see if they were really surrounded.

It now became light, and after the householder's declaration, the situation was now perfectly clear. The cottage looked like a small fortress, and it was no easy thing to get into it. So we should have to force the bandits to move. Having, therefore, assigned to each of my posts its particular target, i.e. some opening in the house, door, window or balcony, I ordered fire to be reopened simultaneously, so that a hail of bullets was poured into the house from all sides. The bandits made a vigorous reply on all sides, and the fight raged fiercely in full view of the population who, attracted by the noise of the firing, were growing every moment thicker on the opposite slope of the valley. The curiosity and interest of the public were so great that the town authorities had to make certain groups move on, because some shots from the bandits on the balcony, aimed high, had come among them.

Suddenly, as I was looking up, I distinctly saw one of the bandits crawling out of the window of the dovecot and up the roof of the house to get to the top and find a better field of fire there. I pointed him out at once and a violent volley went in his direction. The bandit got off unhurt, but one of our bullets broke an arm of a small stone cross that stood at that place on the roof: and the bandit saw this. The bold attempt had meanwhile put my men's backs up and our fire was resumed more hotly than ever. On the other hand, none of us was under any delusion. It was remembered that the bandit Torrigiami, formerly, when surrounded by the police, had first fought gallantly and then committed suicide rather than surrender; and it was thought that Grisafi was of the same mettle. But that was not so. The more savage such men are, the more cowardly.

All at once, as we were still keeping up a hot fire, loud shouts came from inside the cottage: *"N'arrénnemu! N'arrénnemu!"* (we surrender). I was surprised and, suspecting some trick, I replied in a loud voice: "I don't accept!" and turning to my men I shouted: "Continuous fire!" Another hail of bullets penetrated the house at every opening, and the shouts of surrender became desperate. I ordered fire to cease and went to the closed door of the yard, ordering the bandits to lay down their arms, to open the door and come out with their hands up, and giving them two minutes' grace, after which I should break down the door and rush the house by storm without answering for their lives. The two minutes went by in silence: then, quickly breaking in the door, I went into the yard with my officers and men, resolved to put my threat into execution. As we rushed in, however, at the top of a flight of steps that went from the yard to the house Grisafi followed by his four companions, appeared unarmed and with his hands up. It was the end of a reign!

The bandits had excellent military muskets, both 91's and Mausers, the best revolvers, *armes blanches*, field-glasses and a large store of ammunition, much of it with explosive bullets which were particularly dear to Grisafi. I asked him at once why, having lost nobody by death or wounds and still having so much ammunition, he had decided to surrender. He looked at me and made no answer. And at that moment, in the eyes of the man who had shed so much blood and caused so much terror for the last twelve years, I saw the frightened look of a bull that is being led to slaughter.

I shall never forget the scene of the captured band's bringing into the town. Right from the immediate neighbourhood of the cottage the road was lined by parties of onlookers which gradually turned into a large crowd. For a good part of the way the sullen group of bandits went by in a silence of almost overwhelming incredulity. Suddenly the crowd gave tongue. There was such a shout of joy and liberation as I shall never forget. The bandits turned pale and cast down their eyes. Later on, however, one or two of them came to notice again. In fact, some months later, in the big prison at Palermo, Grisafi procured a revolver somehow and killed his prison-companion, the bandit Gallo, on account of some old grudge. A little later Santangelo, who had succeeded in escaping, came back to the district of Sciacca, killed two people and then disappeared.

# Part Two

## From May, 1924, Onwards

I think I have now said enough to express the problem of public safety in Sicily in its proper terms: and if I have attempted to trace the causes of the state of things revealed, I have certainly not intended to assign the responsibility for it. I should never think of putting on a judge's robe, which I have no title or right to assume. Men of action make facts, but do not judge them: they realise how easy it is to be wise after the event. Those who preceded me on this rough road, often staining it with their blood, though ennobling it with their courage, all had one common, single aim—the aim of duty. What caused the undoubted efforts made in the past to peter out was a feeling of listlessness in the minds of the people which seemed refractory even to unusual stimulants. It was not a reality, it was not a fact, but a feeling; yet the past was infected and dominated by it until the day when, on the coming of Fascism, the Duce in person broke the evil spell.

That was in May, 1924. Mussolini came to the island, made personal contact with the people and, though he had never been there before, in a week reached such an understanding of Sicily's soul, needs and grievances as no statesman had ever reached. Moreover, he made himself understood. He told Sicily publicly and solemnly what no statesman had ever yet told her; and for the first time Sicily felt that she, too, was understood. The people asked above all for security, tranquillity and freedom to work; Mussolini promised these things fully and immediately. The hour of liberation had come. In the name and by the will of the Duce action was at last going to be taken. Thus it was that, called to the honour of taking part in it, I returned to Sicily for the third time.

My point of view is very simple. I have never believed that the abnormality of the conditions of public safety in Sicily constituted, in itself, a problem peculiar to the island. I do not say that there was no problem; but it lay in the state of things, in men's minds. It lay, not in what took place, but in the views held about it; it lay, not in the dynamics of criminal offensive, but in the stasis of social defence. This is the only explanation of the fact that such a local, degenerate institution as the Mafia could have prevailed over the conception of the State to the point of creating a state within the State, a régime within a régime; the régime of the Mafia, that is, with its own laws, its own tributes of money and blood, and its own penal sanctions, which completely dominated and exploited the activities of the island, insulting the State and greatly injuring the people, who—with no liberty of choice—the real State being distant and inert and the other state near at hand and operative—had to bow to the latter and submit to its yoke.

One thing at any rate was certain: that there was a permanent excess of criminal activity. Here, as I said at the beginning, lay the real problem. The excess in itself, although unusual, was a common occurrence, observable in all countries and in all times and due to a thousand different reasons which, either by natural exhaustion or as the result of intervention from without, pass away, The problem lay, not in the *existence,* but in the *permanence,* of this excess. It was due to historical causes and particularly to the introduction of Liberal ideas into a society that was unprepared for them. The old vice-regal penal system, though harsh, had been an organic and adequate whole: but the new laws based on the new ideas were inadequate in their action, since the local conditions indispensable to their effectiveness did not yet exist. Moreover, the more liberal tone of the law appeared to the island masses, still uneducated as they were, an inexplicable confession of weakness.

This made the failure of State action inevitable at the outset: and this was particularly serious in its depressing effects upon the mind of the people. Failure ensued, reiterated, persistent and incurable. The people were left defenceless and realised their position. Every man, seeing that the evil persisted, took what steps he could to assure his own interests. Those who were oppressed or threatened came to terms with the criminals; those who had money paid to be left alone, purchasing security for themselves and for their property from the very people who threatened them. And the State found itself excluded from the relations between the sufferers and the malefactors. The Mafia took its place. The country, forced into silence, remained shut into itself, opposing a systematic mutism to investigatory action. What should have been a collaboration in mutual confidence between the authorities and the sufferers was perverted into a source of mutual distrust. The authorities said that it was impossible to act against crime because not only did the people refuse to help them, but the very sufferers favoured the evildoers instead of co-operating with justice. The people and the sufferers, on their side, retorted that it was useless and dangerous to collaborate with the authorities, since the latter could not defend them from the attacks and the reprisals of the criminals. Thus there was a vicious circle; which amounts to saying that nothing was done.

It was a simple question of will, but not everybody saw it so. Reluctance to undertake responsibility, sentimentality and legal formalism needed to be overcome. Either the organs of State action needed to be strengthened with opportune legal provisions or the tendency to legal formalism and jealousy of the executive needed to be overcome by giving full rein to bold initiative. For my own part, though in these matters I respect the sanctity of law, I am, and have always been, for granting free initiative, naturally within the limits of the law, but regarding the law as a guiding principle, not as an obstacle to action.

# My Programme Of Action

The struggle with the Mafia was fought to a finish for the first time under the Fascist regime, but it was not simply police action of a repressive kind. It could not be so, for it contained a moral element which transcended mere police action: and I felt that it ought not to be so, since previous efforts had failed precisely for the reason that they had been repressive in the strictest sense and that they had been conducted as a settling of accounts between the authorities and the criminals in an environment of public mistrust and suspicion. This psychological error had vitiated State action from the beginning. The struggle in its new phase was invigorated both by the impulse of the Duce and by the fact that, under the Fascist conception of the State, the Government was specifically concerned in rendering the existence of the Mafia—an anti-state—impossible. Besides this, a heavy blow was dealt at the Mafia, a little later, by the abolition of the electoral system from which it derived its main source of power and prestige.

Moreover there was a third factor: the whole conscience and will of Sicily were in the fight. This factor, which had always existed below the surface, had for long been underrated and insufficiently made use of: it was a delicate thing, but of the highest value. After my long study of the problem of public safety in relation to Sicily and with my knowledge of the changes which the War had made in the mental evolution of the people, I had become convinced that other methods must be tried. The secret of success lay, I felt sure, in the heart of the Sicilians: but they would give their hearts only to those who could understand and take them at their proper value. The thing, therefore, was to strengthen this determination to the utmost and to throw the entire weight of it into the fight. It was not to be a more or less grandiose police campaign, but a revolt of the people's conscience. There would, it is true, be need for police operations, but these were to be regarded simply as the punishment for crimes that had remained too long unpunished; and their aim would be to facilitate and assist the change of heart in the island itself and to make its conquests permanent.

My programme of action was in accordance with these principles. It is summarised under the following heads:—

1.  The gaining of an immediate and resounding success, such as to break the vicious circle and gain the people's confidence to the side of the State. This meant a decisive attack upon the strongest and most significant of the positions held by the Mafia and the agencies of crime. Success was imperative: audacity meant victory.

2.  Openly to involve the Sicilian people in the action, by executing it in their name.

3.  To give the timid, the disappointed and the discouraged confidence in themselves, in their capacities and in their rights, to create a public state of mind resistant to crime and to give the Mafia, not only a severe blow from without, but a feeling that its environment was against it.

4.  To resist all the power of degenerate *omertà*, while arousing and making use of the pure *omertà* by appealing to the people's sense of pride, their courage, their readiness to resist force by force and to combine against evil, and their love of open and loyal dealing against the tyranny of crime and the old conspiracy of silence.

5.  To set the people free, revive the sense of justice and reassert the authority of the law by proceeding against the authors of many crimes that had been ignored or not been punished.

6. To make a distinction between the Mafia and crime, fighting the latter chiefly in its perpetrators, in its combinations, in its harbours and refuges and in its lines of retreat, but fighting the former not only in the persons of its members, but in its mentality, its prestige, its intimidatory power and in its internal economic system, especially in destroying the net of every kind of interest that formed its connective and protective tissue.

7. To restore to their normal state all the healthily productive activities of the island, so as to set its industries, especially agriculture, on a firm footing, which would be one of the surest safeguards against attempts to return to the past.

8. To create a new spiritual atmosphere, especially by bringing about a direct contact between the people and the State: that is, to stop the interference of the Mafia in all public and private affairs and the spirit of reciprocity and compromise that resulted from it, to put an end to the system by which citizens could not, or would not, approach the authorities except through an intermediary, thus obtaining as a favour what was theirs by right and conferring an entirely unreal power and prestige upon the Mafia.

9. To set about the formation of a new consciousness that should come with time, chiefly, by education, especially of the young, without having too many sentimental illusions about the saving of lost or damaged souls, or the repentance of such as had gone astray. This education was to recognise and make use of the typical traits of the Sicilian character, not to repress them; to turn their innate pride into rebellion against evil tyranny, their passionate nature towards the generous comprehension of other men's needs and weaknesses, their impulsiveness into readiness for action, their exuberance into a reserve of energy, their fatalism into that higher form of Christian resignation which is a conscious and manly resistance to adversity. Even the innate sentiment of

vendetta, which is a source of so much danger, sorrow and blood, can in time be directed towards a profound respect for the personality of others, if it is only approached in the right way.

Such was my programme of immediate action. In certain expert or pseudo-expert quarters my ideas, which I had never concealed, aroused discussion, and they were received with some reserve on three main grounds. First of all, many people regarded the situation as a pure and simple question of the police, and I denied this. Secondly, there was no agreement as to what exactly was meant by the police. The third ground was that, in some people's opinion, it was dangerous to rouse the people to direct resistance against crime and to involve them in an action that should be exclusively one of the State. However, these discussions were all theoretical and only the amateur specialists took part in them. But not all the public at large understood my programme, general attention being mainly concentrated on the vast amount of judicial activity that accompanied the police measures. People became convinced that, as a whole, the struggle was merely a repressive police action in the grand style, of wide extent and particularly brisk in pace.

The Mafia and Co. at once set to work as usual. The ship was leaking badly this time and they sent up the usual S.O.S., but nobody came to the rescue. Besides, the expression on the Duce's face had not been promising: his words, *"ferro e fuoco"* (steel and fire), had been worse. So they had recourse to the usual devices, furbishing them up and perfecting them in my honour. I will give some typical examples. For instance, when I called the people into line and incited them to speak out and give evidence openly and loyally, some protested under their breath that I was encouraging informers. Again, when motor lorries were seen full of unhappy men going to expiate a past of crime, some people protested that the sorry sight was a blot on Sicily's honour: and it seemed to me curious that they should identify Sicily with those who had put themselves outside the pale of law and moral order and declare that the true calumniators of Sicily were themselves the victims of calumny. Again, as soon as repressive action became as intense as the criminal activity it had to repress, a cry of "exaggeration" went up. Indeed, those who were ignorant or absent might have thought our measures strong: but nobody had any idea of the excesses which crime had reached. But the Mafia knew, and played upon the fact with more than its habitual perversion of the truth. I was called a tyrant, an abuser of power, and unjust: so it has always been, and always will be. That is always the cry when the Mafia and crime are attacked. There were cries of persecution, but only on account of the Mafia, as a reflection of its interests in local politics and elections. There were protests on behalf of good government, of public order, or the rights of property, especially the Mafia's property. The Mafia, when touched in this quarter, knows well how to put on the airs of a victim of political persecution. But the game is now played out. Abusive legends grew up about me. One man called me, literally, "a man whose heart was covered with hair," and another simply called me a "wild beast." But I do not wish to be dramatic: and in spite of these legends, I remain what I am. And I can quote ample testimony from men who followed the struggle and published their opinions and impressions while the fight was on, to correct any false opinions. But those who understood me more than any were the people themselves, from whose generous hearts came hundreds of warm expressions of confidence, support and gratitude. Some of these were couched in the most flowery poetry.

While the fight against the Mafia was at its height, a distinguished foreign journalist came to me at Palermo and asked me for details of the measures that were being taken: he seemed to think they involved a regular military campaign with regiments of infantry, squadrons of cavalry, machine guns and other little trifles of that kind. I told him to go round the country and have a look for himself. When he came back a few days later, I asked him what he had seen. "Nothing particular," he said. "The roads and the country were quiet. I saw peasants hard at work, and a few squads of police here and there. I can't understand all the stories I heard."

"I'll tell you," I replied. "The fight is going on here today before your eyes. But you don't see it. It is being fought by those very peasants you saw hard at work in the fields. Each of those men had fought and won, or is going to win, a battle in his heart, in and against himself, or against that part of himself that had remained inert and supine in opposition to crime, whether through fear, or tradition, or habit. Thousands of individual, internal conflicts are going on, though all cannot perceive this, and the total result of them is one single, great and noble action—an action that no forces of crime can resist, because it is the advance of a whole people."

As regards the actual measures that I took, I will be brief. My first act was to create an *interprovincial police service*. I had not been given plenary powers in Sicily: there was no need for that. My specific function was to co-ordinate and direct the activities intended to protect public safety in Sicily towards a single end. My powers were those of the common law, with the additional authorisation to make applicable all over the island the ordinances I had issued as Prefect of Palermo. My plans were such that I did not wish to divide responsibility with anyone, nor could I expect anyone else to assume responsibility for them. I needed, therefore, an instrument directly under my hand, and I made it at once; and it worked by means of groups of police suitably distributed over the island, all directly under my orders. The special instructions that I drew up show what kind of an instrument this was, and I will summarise the interesting points in these.

The interprovincial police service was a special service for the relentless pursuit of crime and untrammelled by considerations of provincial jurisdiction. It was to be autonomous, highly mobile, and so organised that it could conduct operations of the widest scope without dislocating the ordinary local police service. It was to be above all a service of initiative, mobility and action, and to be in all cases self-sufficing. It was to collaborate with local authorities but under arrangements made by its own head office. Its main objects were *(a)* to execute all the necessary operations; *(b)* to assist the action of the local police; *(c)* to create and maintain continuity between the police action in the different provinces; *(d)* to make this action more regular and vigorous, with the aim of attaining a state of satisfactory and permanent tranquillity; and *(e)* to educate the personnel and bring the practice of the police back to the fundamental idea *that all police service must be based on a system of accurate and intense observation, information and investigation.*

The interprovincial police, in their relations with the people, were to be extremely careful to distinguish and isolate criminals, to identify themselves with their locality and attract to themselves the confidence of the people by their resolute assertion of their authority and their efficient action. They were particularly recommended to have a sober demeanour, to be scrupulously correct in carrying out their duties, to respect local customs, to have regard for women, not to persecute the families of those they had to pursue, to keep their word, to be reserved in talking about their duties, to be absolutely silent as regards all who for any reason had confided secrets or information under pledge of secrecy to them, to have personal courage, respect for the law and readiness to lend their services in any capacity, loyally and disinterestedly, wherever they were called for. For the honour of their corps they were to be specially courteous in behaviour, and cordial in their relations with all officials, civil and military, employed in local services.

Where criminals used fire-arms, immediate and energetic reply was to be made with the same till the criminals were captured or had surrendered. Where armed criminals had assembled in a closed place at night, the place was to be closely surrounded so as to prevent all escape, and firing was to be restricted as much as possible to avoid betraying the position of the police. By day fire was to be answered by intense fire, so as to secure the surrender of the criminals or to make an inrush of the police possible.

When following armed criminals in open country, the greatest care was to be had in maintaining open order, so as not to offer a target, specially when the pursuit was over undulating ground: and bunching on the sky-line was to be avoided.

In order to assist the action that was to be taken it was indispensable to provide for the regulation of certain activities that were particularly liable to abuse and to give the police authorities better means of carrying out their functions. To make good deficiencies in the police regulations then in force I issued two ordinances. The first of these more particularly concerned the towns, since it regulated the porters (a rather untrustworthy element, especially at Palermo, where the profession was practically monopolised and controlled by the Mafia), the personnel in general employed in public services (into which undesirable elements often found their way), the employment agencies and middle-men, the practice of *zuinaggio* (the enticing-in of sick persons for profit, particularly prevalent at Palermo, a practice against which all the medical profession had long protested in vain), and the garages and the hiring of motor vehicles in general— motors in the service of armed criminals having already been seen going openly about Palermo. This ordinance, also, made a photograph obligatory on all passports, licences and papers of identity, so as to facilitate the identification of suspects and the search for *latitanti* and all persons wanted by the police. The second ordinance concerned the country districts and regulated the *campieri*, the leasing of land, the goatherds, unauthorised pasturage and the marking of beasts to prevent cattle-raiding. These two ordinances are reproduced textually in the Appendix. Both of them, especially the second which went to the root of the evil, met with general approbation, though a few, as usual, grumbled that they were unconstitutional or dangerous. But here again it was proved that *consensus facit legem* (consent makes law).

# The Bandits Of The Madonie

As I said before, one of the main points of my programme was to obtain a concrete and unequivocal success for the new State action at the beginning—a success which was only to be obtained by attacking and carrying the strongest and most significant position held by the Mafia and crime. Such a position there was; that of the Madonie.

The Madonie are a majestic and picturesque group of mountains which rise upon the north of the island about a third of the distance between Palermo and Messina. Set in this massif or dotted about its slopes, at one time thickly covered with forests of which there are still some imposing traces, there are eleven pretty and characteristic villages. These are Alimena, Bonfratello, Gerace Siculo, Gratteri, Isnello, Castelbuono, Collesano, Polizzi Generosa, Petralia Soprana, Petralia Sottana and Gangi, all of which contain a healthy and vigorous population of farmers and peasants. For more than thirty years however, assisted by the nature of the ground and by the difficulty of communication, the Mafia and the agencies of crime had gained an absolute dominion over the Madonie, in such a way as really to create a state within the State. Every kind of activity, especially agricultural activities, every kind of interest, the most intimate family relations, the public administration, in fact everything, was under the control of the Mafia and the forces of crime whose will was the only law on those mountains; and the Mafia had been assisted in strengthening its hold by the fact that in the past the attempts made to resist it had had no concrete results. And this had conferred such prestige on the Mafia of the Madonie that its superiority was recognized by all the criminals in Sicily.

When I arrived in the province of Palermo the situation in Madonie was very serious and urgent. The whole neighbourhood was completely under the thumb of the Mafia, and this had immediate effects upon the neighbouring districts and the adjacent provinces of Messina, Enna and Caltanissetta; heavy *taglie,* imposed and exacted like regular annual taxes, burdened the landed proprietors; the district itself was practically owned by the bandits who kept it in subjection by their presence and often went about it in an armed band; and there had been disputes and incidents of bloodshed between some of the Madonie groups and some groups belonging to the province of Caltanissetta on questions of supremacy. Altogether, there were present in the Madonie about 130 armed *latitanti,* centring round three small groups which were led by the bandits Andalaro, Ferrarello, Dino and certain lesser men. The centre of the movement was Gangi, a very picturesque village which completely covers a small mountain side from top to bottom like a great hood embroidered with windows and balconies and broken up by sharp roofs and corners.

A particular feature of the situation was that this was not a case of wandering banditry. The bandits of the Madonie, or at least their leaders, had made quite a position for themselves. They owned houses, some even had a farm, land and cattle, and they had become accustomed to a comfortable and sedentary life. They did not normally move about the country. They only united and went about in armed bands for special enterprises or to exact tribute from refractory landowners. For the most part they stayed at home in Gangi. By way of precaution, however, every one of them had made, underneath, above or at the side of his dwelling-place, a comfortable hiding-place conveniently furnished which was approached by ways and by openings that had been very cleverly concealed. There were a good many of these, certainly quite enough to hold all of them. At the same time, the lay-out of the village of Gangi, while it was favourable to these arrangements through the ease with which internal communications could be made and ways of entry and exit be concealed, made it extremely difficult to identify these details from the outside; so that the police had never been able to obtain even an approximate plan of the village. There had been on the spot for some time a gallant police official, the police-commissioner, Spano, with a force of picked *carabinieri* and police agents.

Such being the state of things, I decided to act at once, all the more since the time of year—it was winter—would be a good ally, and since decision and rapidity were necessary for the success of the operation. I began at a considerable distance off by moving about groups of police with obvious frequency inside a zone which surrounded the Madonie at a distance of twenty kilometers. This demonstration was necessary to keep the bandits at whom I was aiming from leaving their district without disturbing them. They gave no sign of anxiety: things were evidently going as I had foreseen. In a very few days the movement at a distance became more intense. It came a little closer and took the appearance of an almost circular girdle with its centre at Gangi. This time it was a real distant blockade. Even this did not disturb the bandits.

They evidently thought that it was one of those usual operations called *battues* to which the police sometimes had recourse in the search for *latitanti* and for the purpose of reassuring the country people. And, as it was beginning to get cold, they began to flock quietly into Gangi to take up their quarters there.

At the first vague news of this, while maintaining the distant blockade, I suddenly entered the stretch of country between it and the village of Gangi, occupying the farms and places that contained property or friends of the bandits with independent groups of police, and declaring them all under sequestration. This time the bandits became anxious, because the objective of the operation was becoming clear. But now it was too late for them to act. For them to leave the village and take to the woods would mean running into the groups of police that were dotted about in occupation of the farm buildings and in communication with one another, or else into the more distant circle of blockaders. So they did what I thought they would do.

In the impossibility of finding any other way out, the bandits of Gangi shut themselves up in their comfortable, secure, and inviolable hiding-places in the village. While waiting on events they all disappeared into the bowels of the village, as though sucked up by a colossal sponge. Although it took place silently, this movement did not escape the police-commissioner, Spano, who gave me immediate notice of it. I then removed the distant blockade which had now become useless, and in a single night, with a strong force of police agents, *carabinieri* and voluntary militia for national safety which had been specially sent from Palermo, I completely enveloped the houses of Gangi by an unbroken line of armed men. This line had contact with the outermost houses and precluded any entrance or exit.

But that was not enough. I was determined not to give the bandits the honour of arms. I had no intention that crime should once more get a halo of prestige, of courage and even of martyrdom after a combat with the police. Not only did I intend to win, that is, to hand the bandits over to justice, but I also wanted to give the people a tangible proof of the cowardice of criminals. Therefore, as soon as I had information that the surrounding of the village was complete, I telegraphed to the mayor of Gangi in these words: "I summon the *latitanti* who are in your territory to give themselves up within twelve hours, on the lapse of which I shall proceed to extreme measures. Please have this published by means of criers." Some people who saw the telegram before I sent it observed that I was taking some risk. That was true, but I wished that the assertion of State power with which the fight began should be absolute, i.e. an assertion of moral force and prestige. On the other hand, if the bandits did not give themselves up, I should win the game in a different way, but just as quickly and decisively. At all events, my telegram was spread abroad through the astonished and deserted streets of Gangi to the sound of the crier's drum and his voice came to the hidden bandits like a challenge.

Some hours of uncertainty ensued, and in order to precipitate events I gave orders that, while the blockade of the village was maintained, the police should enter all the houses of the bandits and the *latitanti* and occupy them permanently. These orders were carried out at once without incident, and the bandits, in their undiscoverable hiding-places, heard the continual tramp of the men on guard sounding heavily above them in their own houses. They made no sign, there was no attempt to resist, or to break out. The bandits, obviously surprised, divided and thrown out of their bearings, were not in good form. I took advantage of this to depress their spirits still further by ordering that some cattle which had evidently been stolen and had been seized on their property should be slaughtered and publicly sold to the people at bankrupt prices together with other produce of the same origin. This was immediately done: the echo of it reached the hiding-places and had its effect. The cup was full: besides their loss they also suffered the insult. There was nothing left for them but to make up their minds, either to die like rats in their holes or to come out. But outside there was I with my "extreme measures" and dangerous intentions; and the air was unhealthy. And people began to laugh at these terrible bandits who, though laden with arms and ammunition and distinguished by a past of bloodshed and conflicts with the police, stayed like rabbits in their burrows without the courage even to put their noses out to resist the havoc that was being played with their property. It was a ridiculous situation; and doubtless the bandits began to feel it, if only obscurely. And they also realised that, when the first moment had gone by in which a violent reaction might have had some value and some result, it was no longer possible to make an armed *sortie* against people who had laughed in their faces. The ridiculous has the same results as panic, and panic is a close relation of fear: and fear increases in proportion to the square of the time. And so it was that the famous bandits of the Madonie made up their minds.

All of a sudden, one by one, they crawled out of their various hiding-places and gave themselves up to the police—all of them, without striking a single blow. And as they went by, a Homeric burst of laughter exploded behind the men who had so often left a trail of sorrow, tears and blood in their wake. Only one of them, perhaps suffering from an acute attack of historical reminiscence, did not give himself up at once, declaring that he felt the spirit of Brutus (with a capital B) arising in his heart; but at the critical moment he forgot his history and joined the herd of his less Roman but more practical companions. Another, after having given himself up, pretended to be ill and succeeded in escaping from his own house where he was in custody by a mysterious secret passage. He took to the open country with the declared intention of obtaining a bloodthirsty revenge. The same evening, however, when this had become known a large group of armed inhabitants of the place—and this was a very significant and unheard-of action—came to the local authority and put themselves at its disposition for the immediate pursuit of the unhappy man who, seeing what was afoot, gave himself up again definitely. The only gesture made was that of the chief Ferrarello, a man of sixty years old, who, though he surrendered in a moment of panic like all the rest, hanged himself for shame as soon as he got to prison.

The rapidity of this operation and truly inglorious end of the bandits of the Madonie, who had covered themselves with such a terrible aura of prestige and legend, had immediate and profound repercussions over the whole of Sicily. From that moment, as though affected by a depressing and contagious impulse, the *latitani* in circulation were unable to hold out any longer and came to give themselves up after a simple summons. Among others there was one, belonging to the province of Agrigento, who had been guilty of homicide and for whom there had been for some time a hot pursuit; and this man one fine day wrote me a flowery letter adorned with some poetry to express his sympathy and to declare that he would come and give himself up personally to me. I asked him to come by all means; and since he was wandering about the country, I sent the letter to the following address: "Signor C----*latitante*, R-- (his home village)'

It sometimes happens that letters do not reach their destination, but this one, in spite of the uncertain residence of the addressee, arrived punctually. One morning, just as I was preparing to leave the house, an official came to tell me that a short time before an individual of a fierce aspect had come to the door and asked to see me. When he was told that I could not see visitors at that hour, the individual had made a rude answer, and a sort of dispute had ensued followed by the intervention of a police patrol, the hold-up of the individual, his identification as the *latitante*, C- (the man who wrote the letter), his immediate arrest and his consignment to the police-station.

"Set him free at once," I said to the official, and, at his look of more than legitimate surprise, I repeated the order. C- was immediately and very reluctantly released. But I knew very well the kind of man I had to deal with. It was a case of loyalty for loyalty. A quarter of an hour later C—— came to the Prefecture and asked to be shown in to me. He came in, kissed my hand, declaimed some phrases, probably verses, in my honour and went away with the blessings of Heaven which, represented in this case by two *carabinieri*, were waiting for him at the main prison.

In the general *débacle* of the *latitanti* and bandits of the island there remained one last point of resistance. This was the Sacco group, composed sometimes of three and sometimes of four *latitanti*, which operated in the eastern zone of the province of Agrigento. The gallant corps of *carabinieri* took charge of them, and after an able and close pursuit led by Captain Romeo, a veteran in the fight against crime, they overcame them by surprise in a bloody conflict in which they showed all the valour of their heroic traditions.

The fall of the bandits of the Madonie made a strong impression upon popular imagination which showed itself, among other things, in the form of occasional poems which I need not quote. But this proved that I was right in thinking that the conscience, heart and will of the whole people was in the struggle against the Mafia. In what manner it was regarded by the head of the Government I knew; but the people were clearly informed of it when I published the following telegram which reached me on the 6th January, 1926:

"*Prefect Mori, Palermo*. During my voyage in Sicily I said in a public square before a large and enthusiastic crowd of people that the noble population of Sicily must be liberated from the grip of rural crime and of the Mafia. I see that after clearing out the province of Trapani you are continuing your work magnificently in the Madonie. I express to you my great and lively delight and I exhort you to continue to the end without regard for anyone, high or low. Fascism which has healed Italy of so many wounds will, if necessary, cauterise with fire and hot iron the wound of crime in Sicily. Five million hard-working and patriotic Sicilians must no longer be oppressed, held to ransom, robbed or dishonoured by a few hundred criminals. This problem must also be, and shall be, solved. I authorise you to make this dispatch public in the local newspapers. Mussolini."

The success of the operation in the Madonie, besides bringing the people to our side with renewed confidence, profoundly impressed the Mafia and the criminal classes. It was necessary to take immediate advantage of this and to remove any illusions or hopes that might be left to them. With this object, a few days later, at a solemn and imposing gathering of Fascists which was held at the Teatro Massimo in Palermo, which was packed with spectators of every class, I made the following declaration:—

"The offensive which has now been fully launched will be pushed inexorably to the finish without regard for anybody. To those who stand on the other side I say these few but solemn words. It is useless to be under the illusion that this is merely a puff of wind. It will be a regular cyclone which will carry away everything, root and branch. It is useless to put hope in the failure or imperfection of the law. The law will be made or improved or corrected; and in any case, wherever it may fail or be imperfect, there *we* shall be with convincing arguments. It is useless to put hope in judicial abstractions which have sometimes ruled in the courts of justice. . . . It is useless to rely upon the existence of contracts. All that has been obtained by compulsion is invalid *(I meant here to allude to the contracts for the lease of land extorted by violence).* It is useless to rely upon the prejudices and the fears of other people. Prejudice has now been overcome, and fear, its livid companion, has gone over to the enemy, with arms and baggage, at the double. It is useless to hope for more or less interested or charitable intervention. This is an old-fashioned method which would expose those who use it to ridicule, or even worse. It is useless to think of a return to the attack. Dead men do not return. On the other hand, to confront that past, we are here at our posts, resolved to remain there 'so long as the harm and the shame remains.' And the rising generation will be against that past: I mean, the multitude of noisy tousle-headed boys who are now rolling about in the sun and making the fair countryside of this burning island merry with their cries and from whom you unhappy men on the other side will never again be able to draw new recruits: for we again shall be surrounding it with watchfulness and arms. . . . Against that past, finally, by the will of the Duce, through the enthusiasm of a man called Giuriati (then Minister of Public Works) and the work of capable pioneers there is rising an insurmountable fence—a network of roads, aqueducts and works of land drainage.

"There is, therefore, nothing left for you, unhappy men on the other side, but the inexorable dilemma which I put to you now for the last time: either to redeem yourselves loyally through honest labour or to die. Those whom the cap fits should put it on, and quickly. We know what we have to do, and we are doing it."

The Teatro Massimo of Palermo was a witness of the overwhelming enthusiasm with which the Fascists and the people greeted my words, And the formidable roar that went up from the masses gathered there must have reached those of the other side like the dreadful knell of their last hour.

# Rounding Up

From words I passed immediately to deeds. The people's attitude, although still only potential, was clear: I had only to give it actuality. In conjunction with the local police forces, the groups of inter-provincial police, which I had distributed, as I said, among the districts where crime was most prevalent and whose activities—although they enclosed the main centres of crime in a complete network—I had hitherto deliberately limited to that of guarding and protecting the districts, now entered decisively on their specific and predetermined functions. They made a thorough contact with their environment, and in the new atmosphere of increasing confidence attracted to their side the desire for freedom that was already arising in the heart of the people.

The result of this was a kind of general spiritual osmosis by which all that for long years had been locked in the bottom of their hearts and had formed an evil ferment which poisoned the life of families—deaths unavenged, sorrows without a name, obscure tragedies, formidable losses, impositions, vexations, injustices, and terrible obsessions—all came to light in the form of clear narrations, open denunciations, precise indications, and bold evidence. The compulsory *omertà* which had wrapped the island in silence, and in which short-sighted people had often seen nothing but a mark of degeneration, ceased at once; and there was brought to light a grievous tale of long unpunished crime for which it was now time to bring the perpetrators to strict account. With the power of the State present and at work, with a vigilant and active government, and with the light of a patriotic ideal shining for all to see, Sicily found herself again. Rising up against her evil genius, the evil domination and the

163

evil legends, in the name of her dignity, of her right and of her long agony, she declared loudly and publicly: *"J'accuse."*

In a short time, the inter-provincial police had collected an imposing amount of evidence against the Mafia and other criminals which formed a starting point for the proceedings of the judicial police that I shall shortly mention. But before doing anything else, in accordance with the plan that I had marked out, I availed myself of this evidence to strike at the Mafia in the persons of its leading agents, with the aim both of destroying its prestige and of disorganising thereby the general staff of crime in Sicily. The fall of the bandits of the Madonie had already revealed the existence of a widespreading association for criminal purposes which had obtained a stranglehold on that large district. The people, when freed from it at last, told all. The landed proprietors who had for so long been oppressed and held to tribute took their position decisively beside the authorities; and the sad story of the tragic episodes that had happened in the Madonie finally came to light, documented and proved in every particular. More than a hundred and fifty people were arrested on charges of association to commit crime or of murder, blackmail, robbery, cattle-stealing and so forth.

While this was going on in the Madonie, the most authoritative, redoubtable and active agents of the Mafia were struck down one by one with their respective groups of satellites in the districts round Palermo and elsewhere.

There was no possibility of escape. Since their strength had only lain in other people's fears and in the inaction of the State, the people's impetuous uprising and the activity of the government now annihilated them. Hemmed in between the police and a revulsion of the people round them, dismayed and panic-stricken, they fell like flies, with no other gesture of resistance but a feeble attempt at flight to well-concealed hiding-places. They were all struck down; and at the door of each one of them justice laid a specific burden of clear and precise accusation drawn up by those who had hitherto been the victims. In some cases the arrests had serious consequences. For instance, when the head of the Mafia in the district of Mistretta, who had been particularly respected and feared over a large part of Sicily, was arrested, there were found in his possession about ninety letters which gave away all the threads of a huge association for criminal purposes which worked in the district of the Caronie bordering the Madonie on the east. On the Madonie the Mafia was organised and worked in armed bands; but on the Caronie the situation was different. There the Mafia had formed itself into a regular tribunal and operated by passing sentences which meant blackmail, cattle-raiding, robbery, and the suppression of all who refused to pay or made themselves troublesome. The letters seized, although written in a kind of conventional language, were regrettably clear in their meaning. Indeed, that tribunal had beaten the record for activity. The number of sentences it had passed in a few years was really remarkable. The result was more than two hundred arrests and their relegation to the Assize Court. And so the greater and smaller strongholds of the Mafia fell thus early to the ground with a crash which gave the people a clear and unmistakable feeling that we were acting in earnest.

It was above all else indispensable to create this feeling, because there were still certain districts that had been made sceptical by the memory of other conflicts in other times in which the intervention of the State against criminal activity in the island, although on a large scale, had only been directed against ordinary criminals, that is to say, against those who only acted at the behest of others. The Mafia, at whose behest they acted, was at those times too intimately mixed up in local politics to be easily and effectively struck at. All the same, while the strong positions of the Mafia were tumbling down as we have seen, I took particular pains to act resolutely against crime in general on the basis of the evidence which had been collected.

There ensued the so-called *retate* (rounds-up). Some people called them the "famous" rounds-up; and other people the "usual" rounds-up. In this connection some explanation is perhaps needed, if only as regards my personal responsibility, since the system of rounds-up has often been condemned in my hearing as an abuse of police methods as obvious as it is ineffective, not to speak of its serious and pernicious consequences. The *retate* (the simultaneous arrest of a large number of criminals) were carried out by me in Sicily upon special principles, varying with the times, and with various, but in every case well-defined aims. Thus, for example, there were times in Sicily when the activity of crime became so acute simultaneously in several districts as to make it impossible, in view of the number and rapid succession of the crimes committed, to attempt to investigate single cases. There simply was no time to do so. Therefore, one had either to remain inactive and in observation waiting to act until after the intensity had died down, or to act in the most adequate way. And since the former principle could obviously lead to nothing conclusive, I adopted the second. That is to say, I simultaneously removed from circulation all the suspicious characters in the district; I collected all the more or less vague proofs and indications that could be collected in those times of fear and I handed them all over to the judicial authorities with the certain conviction, however, that the case would come to nothing for want of proof. But meanwhile the access of criminal activity ceased and the martyred countryside had a little respite. It was simply a temporary device, but it was that or nothing. At other times it happened—particularly during the harvest or the seasonal fairs—that in certain districts the activity of crime took such form and intensity as very seriously to endanger the carrying of the harvest and the movement of animals. Numerous groups of armed criminals would steal waggon-loads of grain by the dozen and animals of every kind by the hundred. It was perfectly useless and materially impossible to set up a service of surveillance which should be adequate to the needs of the situation. So there was nothing left but simultaneously to remove from circulation all individuals in these districts who were suspected of specific activity, to collect all possible evidence against them and hand this over to the judicial authorities, although without any illusion that, in the predominant state of terror, the preliminary examination would result in sufficient proof to convict the malefactors. But meanwhile the movement of animals and, above all, the flow of grain from the outlying estates to the collecting centres went on at full speed and undisturbed.

Again, it sometimes happened that after long, careful and close inquiry we had succeeded in collecting strong evidence against numerous individuals who had been guilty of crimes committed some time before. However, the state of the flagrancy having elapsed, it was not legally possible for the instruments of the judicial police to act on their own initiative. Under the ordinary criminal procedure the collected evidence should have been transmitted to the judicial authorities, who would then take action as they were competent to do after having followed the prescribed procedure (interrogations, confrontations, etc.), which meant that they could only act after having raised the alarm sufficiently to render all the criminals in that particular district immediately undiscoverable, and in consequence to induce all those who had given denunciations, indications, testimony, etc., to retract all they had given. In order to avoid this it was necessary to create a state of flagrancy which should allow the instruments of judicial police to act directly. This was obtained by formulating the offence of "association for criminal purposes," particularly on the ground that the same individuals frequently committed the same crime. This was a permanent state of crime and, therefore, flagrant; and on this basis we proceeded to make a sudden and simultaneous round-up with all the necessary subsidiary action and denunciation to the judicial authorities. It is superfluous to say that invariably, as we foresaw, the charge of association for criminal purposes fell at the preliminary examination, but the individual crimes remained, and the guilty remained also.

And this makes it perfectly clear that the so-called rounds-up of former times, far from being blind actions taken merely for outward effect, as short-sighted observers thought, were dictated by definite exigencies and based upon careful consideration. This, at least, was true as regards myself.

The rounds-up, however, which marked the last stage of the struggle had an aspect all of their own. It was not a case of temporarily removing from circulation suspected persons on charges which it was known beforehand could not be definitely proved; it was a case of striking down criminals against whom injured persons and witnesses had furnished positive, concrete and investigated proofs of specific responsibility for individual crimes. It was not a question of arriving inductively at the existence of associations for criminal purposes for purposes of procedure; but it was a case of striking at crime in its traditional manifestations and its associated activities of which we had evident and tangible proof. It was not a case of giving, in some way or other, a certain period of respite to the people by restraining as best we could, by temporary devices or by temporary stoppages, the spread of criminal activity; it was a case of cutting off crime altogether, of giving tranquillity and security to the people, of reviving the sense of justice, of putting an end to a long and troubled period of impunity and of asserting once more the power and prestige of the State. Therefore, I adopted the course of action most suitable to my purpose. I took special care to avoid sending a host of criminals into hiding, which would not only have been a serious danger to the safety of the countryside, but, by renewing the sensation of the fear in the heart of the people, would have inevitably led to the withdrawal of popular confidence and produced immediately a weakening effect upon the consistency and the solidity of our collected evidence. My action had therefore to be taken suddenly, aggressively and simultaneously at different and distant points over well-defined districts and set in motion from without. It had three phases:

(1) Quiet, silent and careful investigation and search to collect all the necessary details of identification and personal responsibility based on written, spoken, signed and tested denunciations and testimonies.

(2) The temporary abandonment of the district that had thus been sounded with the aim of not alarming the criminals; the

examination of the collected details, and the precise geographical delimitation of the district. In this connection it must be observed that from the very first moment the existence of large and varied associations of criminals each working in its own district was revealed.

(3) A sudden invasion of the selected districts from the outside. That is to say, the district, however large it might be, was invested in a single night by a force that had been cautiously concentrated on the spot at the opportune moment. Simultaneously, in the villages and the countryside that had been occupied, all the criminals against whom proof existed were handed over to justice, and together with them all persons who were in any way implicated or suspected. This made the sending of a large number of criminals into hiding impossible, for in a single night the whole of the criminals in the district were in our hands. There followed a rapid examination by the officials of the judicial police. This was the first sifting: and a certain number of arrested persons came out of it unscathed. All the rest were handed over to the competent judicial authorities.

These operations were carried out in considerable numbers and on a large scale: and the rapidity with which they succeeded one another and the exactness of the evidence on which they were based completely strangled the criminal associations which for so many years had flourished with impunity. And the whole island raised a hymn of liberation.

Much has been said about these police operations, and in particular there has been a good deal of exaggeration as to the number of arrests. Of course, three hundred, four hundred or five hundred arrests must make a certain impression: but two things must be borne in mind. In the first place, that each operation covered four, five or sometimes more villages at the same time; and in the second place, that they were the result of a long period of criminal activity. Three hundred arrests carried out in all in five villages each of five thousand persons, for crimes committed in the course of ten years, does not really represent anything abnormal. The abnormality was simply to be found in the impunity which had lasted ten years.

# The People Come Into Line

As we have just seen, the traditional and compulsory *omertà* having been overcome, the people of Sicily, seized with an impulse for freedom, were every day joining more closely with us in common action. But that was not enough for me. There were still, as may be easily understood, the uncertain, the timid, the doubtful, and the wobblers: there were above all those who, remembering the past, were anxious as to what would happen when our operations ceased, since this would leave them exposed to the reprisal of all the criminals whom they had denounced to the authorities or against whom they had given evidence. There were certain old-fashioned states of mind to be overcome, and there were certain *repentant thieves* for the occasion, to be unmasked. In these circumstances, if the people had been left to themselves for a moment, they would have fallen once more under the old yoke. It was necessary, therefore, to raise their spirits to a higher temperature and to give the heart of Sicily consciousness of its own strength, of its own courage, and of its own capacity; to give the population the clear notion of their own rights and their own duty; and to bring about that formidable movement of resistance which would overcome every obstacle by its own impetus and give the fight against crime the character of a determined civic act of manly self-liberation.

While the operations of which I have spoken were proceding with ruthless continuity, I made personal contact with the people of the districts who had most suffered from crime, and visited every village to bring to all, especially the gallant, honest and healthy-minded mass of the peasants, the word of faith and solidarity in the fight. At my call the peasants of Sicily gathered in thousands, listened to my words and sent up a formidable battle cry. And they were glad to see me; they called me the *prefetto contadino*, and they shouted this name with such fervour that the mere memory of it moves me. And all around me, even in remote places which the voice of the government had never yet reached and where up to that moment the Mafia had held absolute sway, there were imposing demonstrations of insurrection and revolt. At my words, upon hills and plains where hitherto mere hesitation to obey the command of the Mafia had been visited with death, there rose for the first time from the peasant masses, powerfully and irrepressibly, that cry which fear had held locked in every man's bosom: "Death to the Mafia!"

My arguments were few but weighty: they were clearly expressed and perfectly understood. I told them that they must react directly against crime by every means, including arms; that they must consider reaction against crime which threatened the life and property of citizens, not only as a right, but above all as a duty; since the citizen's life is vowed to his fatherland and private property is an element in national wealth that all must work to safeguard. They listened to my words. There had already been some cases of direct reaction against crime and other cases occurred. And these were rewarded by the Government with the medal for civic valour. I made the presentation of these medals a special pretext for speaking personally to the people.

The first man to be decorated was a peasant of Bisacquino, where I went myself to pin the medal to his breast: and there I spoke to the mass of peasants who were gathered to witness this ceremony words of encouragement and patriotism, reminding them that the actions for which the medal had been conferred were worthy of a Sicilian and an agriculturist, that the resistance to crime was the right and duty of every citizen, that the fight against the Mafia and crime in general would be carried on to the end, and that it could not be carried on if the population remained an inert spectator. The redemption of Sicily, I told them, must come through her own sons. I spoke to the same effect at Castronuovo and many other places, and I always spoke to the peasants with the same rough directness with which I used to speak to my soldiers in the field when I gave them the usual Sunday lecture. The peasants understood me no less well than the soldiers; they understood me like Sicilians, like honest men and like *men* in the true sense of the word. The whirlwind that I desired was let loose, and it made the air unbreathable for criminals, parasites, those who protected crime and those who profited by it. The downfall of the Mafia and crime was complete; the old dark legends were wiped out; and everywhere men began to breathe a new air.

And I will tell one typical episode: A few kilometers from Palermo there is a large village called Misilmeri, thickly inhabited by a population of strong and hardworking peasants where, for a long time past, the Mafia and crime had been dominant and all kinds of violence had been committed. In 1921, when Fascism was dawning and there were a few signs here and there of reaction against crime, a young man of the place, called Mariano De Caro, had been treacherously assassinated simply for having openly shown a hostile feeling to the Mafia and an intention to stand up to them. A group of young students, acting in his name, kept alive in the village the flame of rebellion; but the neighbourhood, as a whole, seemed to be still mistrustful and to be impervious to any investigation or approach.

I went to Misilmeri more than once and spoke to the people; but it was pointed out to me by someone that, even in their demonstrations of assent and applause, the general aspect of the crowd seemed so unexpressive as almost to give the impression of a general state of insensibility. Such indeed was the appearance; but I felt that the reality must be quite different. I was sure that the long tyranny of crime had trained the whole population to hide their feelings under a motionless countenance, and that passionate hearts like those of the Sicilians could not possibly help being affected, even in Misilmeri, by the breath of revolt that was blowing throughout the island. I wished to put this to the test and in such a way as to convince the sceptics.

There happened to be a distinguished pianist passing through Palermo on a concert tour, and he had his own pianoforte, a very solid and sonorous instrument. I asked him to give a concert to the population of Misilmeri in the public square of the village and to play such pieces as he thought would be most suitable for the taste of that very novel public. The pianist, Maestro Boasso, understood me perfectly and consented with enthusiasm. So the piano was placed on a special platform in the middle of the piazza of Misilmeri; and the population was invited to attend. They came accordingly and stood round the platform in a rather distant circle, silent, emotionless, cool and impassible. The pianist began to play, and played his best. The sun was beginning to set, and the deep and sonorous notes of the piano spread through the air in the solemn melancholy of the hour like a strange melody, now fierce and now caressing, now stimulating and now soothing. The crowd, accustomed to the metallic din of rustic bands, was completely charmed. Slowly, imperceptibly, they came nearer to the platform and stood round it in earnest fascination. Their faces lost their stiffness, lit up and became mild; a faint smile through half-open lips made their brown faces gleam and many eyes glistened as though with tears. And when the pianist had finished, the most enthusiastic applause broke out. The Sicilian heart, overcome by emotion, had revealed itself. Once more I had been right; the impassibility of the population had not been insensibility, but simply self-defence.

I had only to continue the good work. And to begin with, in accordance with the desire expressed to me by the local Fascists, I consented that a stone to the memory of Mariano De Caro should be publicly put up in Misilmeri with a solemn public ceremony. The ceremony took place before all the population of Misilmeri and the neighbouring villages amid great enthusiasm. It was a proud and open stand to arms against the Mafia and against crime. At the end of the ceremony, as I was coming off the platform, somebody expressed to me his fear that the stone might be defaced by criminals. But a little later, as I was passing through the crowd which was intently reading and commenting on the inscription— and this ended with the words: *"a memoria— ad onore— a monito"* (for memory, for honour, for warning)—I overheard the following short dialogue:

"What does *'monito'* mean?" a young fellow asked his neighbour.

"It means," the other answered with a firm and meaning look, *"significa ca cu tocca ccà ci sata a testa"* (that anyone who touches it will get his head cut off).

The stone was evidently very well regarded.

Such, in short, was my action of propaganda and incitement against crime. Naturally, there was no lack of commentators and critics. And there were some who thought it extremely dangerous. Dangerous it certainly was—for the criminals. At all events, it was the only thing to do short of going back to the past and fishing out of the lumber room the vice-regal decree of the second half of the sixteenth century in which, among other things, it says:

"The Captain, on receiving notice of any of the above-mentioned crimes or criminals shall at once summon together his men at arms. He shall go out with them without delay, and shall take information of what has occurred at the hand of the Chief Notary, or of one of his commissaries duly approved and matriculated, and with all speed shall set out in pursuit of the criminals, faring to within thirty miles round the city or place whither it is known or it is supposed that the evil-doers have fled, crying out himself from time to time: *'Fuora, fuora. Piglia i Malandrin'* (come out, come out, and catch the rogues)."

It does not seem, however, that, in spite of the necessarily strong lungs of the captains, this device was very successful. For, if this decree has come to us down the centuries, the rogues have come too.

# *The Campieri*

I have already told in the preceding pages what the *campieri* were, and how by their means the dominion of the Mafia and the whole movement of rural crime was established on the large country estates. For this reason the question of the *campieri* gave particular anxiety to all who had to do with public safety in Sicily. Various remedies for the abuses were suggested: from the complete suppression of the *campieri* and the substitution for them of sworn guards, duly authorised and recognised as agents of public safety, to their weeding out and subsequent conversion into auxiliary agents of private police. None of these suggestions, however, seemed to be practicable or to hit the mark. Therefore, I determined to change the tactics.

It was above all necessary to weed out the personnel and eliminate those who had been guilty of offences, the militant *mafiosi* and the men who had been imposed by the Mafia, but at the same time to preserve the figure of the *campiere* in its traditional form and to bring them into our service as irregulars, as vedettes and as *arditi* for social defence, leaving them, that is, freedom of initiative and action, but only in contact with and in subordination to, the police authorities and in co-operation among themselves for the direct defence, even by force of arms, against crime. They were to have no special caps, no uniform, no special names or privileges. The *campiere* was to remain what he had always been: a man of special capacity, of physical strength, of personal courage and professional loyalty, capable of standing up alone against criminals and of facing by himself the most dangerous situations, but without any formal regulations to hamper him and with the fullest liberty to choose his own methods.

I began with the decree which I have given in full elsewhere, and I soon succeeded in weeding out the personnel. I got rid of the dangerous men and the undesirables, and the remainder made a rough and gallant crew, excellently adapted, if put on the right lines, for the purposes of the fight. It was only necessary to make their minds up.

With this end in view, by a simple summons sent to each of them, I called them all together on the morning of a feast day in a wide open space near Roccapalumba. It was the first time that anything of the kind had happened; and perhaps in some of their minds there was a memory of the famous "three heaps" by which an end had been put to the ancient mounted police. Anyhow they all came, thirteen hundred of them. There were only two missing, and that on the proved ground of sickness. I took with me to the meeting-place an army chaplain three times decorated for valour, Don Ribaudo.

The mass of *campieri* whom I found on the spot, mostly armed and on horseback, were a magnificent picture of strength and vigour. I first inspected them, and then I made them all gather closely round a rock which rose in the middle of the open space and upon which a very modest altar had been prepared. From this low elevation I spoke a few short, rough and plain words. I said that it was easy to understand why in the past, seeing the insufficiency of State power, the owners of landed property had had to look for *campieri* in the Mafia and to submit to receiving orders from the Mafia as to whom they should employ, but that now that the State was vigilant, present and operating, it must never happen again. I added that the *campiere* would keep his traditional figure and function; but I pointed out that he must be a respectable man, of courage and honour, ready even to give his life in defence of what had been entrusted to his care. And I declared that crime could only be put down by immediate and prompt reaction, without compromise of any kind, in full solidarity between comrades and in obedience to the authorities of public safety. I ended by reading them the formula of an oath which every *campiere* would have to swear:—

"I swear to be faithful to the King and to his royal successors, loyally to obey the State and the laws of the State, to carry out my duty as a man of honour and conscience, and to defend the goods and persons entrusted to my care with all my strength, in accordance with the law, with right and with morality, with absolute thoroughness, in loyal solidarity with my comrades and in strict obedience to the authorities who are responsible for the protection of public safety."

My words were followed with evident and intense emotion by the mass of men. More than one of those rough fellows shed tears. No sooner had I read the words of the oath than there was a general rush forward as a prelude to a shout of assent. I motioned for silence, and then said these words: "I have read you the words of the oath, but the moment has not yet come to swear. I want you first of all to look into you own minds and think well, each one of you, what you mean to do. The oath taken here in front of the altar will be doubly sacred and hold you forever. Not only that, but it may cost you your lives. Think it over well. I give you the time which it takes to say a Mass. While the priest says Mass I shall not look at you. If any man wishes to go away, let him go; I shall not know who he is. Those who remain will take the oath." Amid deep general emotion, and under a flaming sun, the priest with blue ribbons bearing silver stars upon his breast said Mass, and followed it by some noble words of faith and redemption. None of the men had gone away. I then came forward, and read the words of the oath again. With a powerful and unanimous cry the crowd of *campieri* answered: "I swear!"

So another legend fell to the ground. Thirteen hundred brave and gallant men came over *en bloc* to our side and into the forces of social defence: and the Mafia lost at a blow one of its strongest supports. For three long hours, under the blazing sun, the *campieri* stayed to put their signatures to the oath. And they honoured that signature. A few days later, in fact, three *campieri* attacked with rifles three malefactors whom they had surprised upon their own territory as they were driving some oxen which they had stolen elsewhere. They dragged them to the barracks of the *carabinieri* and handed them over to justice. A few weeks later another old *campiere,* who in time past had probably helped wanted men and bandits a hundred times, suspected that there was a *latitante* hidden in a hut on the estate entrusted to his care. So he got together some comrades, surrounded the place, took the *latitante* by surprise, bound him hand and foot and sent for the *carabinieri* to hand him over to them. He then informed his employer of what had happened in a letter wherein his primitive mind expressed itself in a kind of hymn of redemption. A little time after this, in the neighbourhood of a farm on one of the estates in the interior which had a very bad reputation, a visiting patrol was one evening treacherously assailed by rifle shots which luckily did not find their target. Neither the immediate nor the subsequent investigations of the officials or of the police who afterwards came up had any results. The occurrence, however, was too serious to be left unpunished. I sent another police official to the spot with definite orders. When he reached the farm, the official found an old woman and interrogated her. At first she gave evasive replies, but finally she gave way to the pressing inquiries of the official and recounted what had happened, mentioning the name of the person who had fired upon the patrol. It was necessary to secure him, but nobody in the police knew him. At this point the official had an idea. He called the *campiere* of the estate to one side and asked him: "Were you at Roccapalumba?," alluding to the meeting at which the *campieri* swore the oath.

"Yes," answered the *campiere,* "and I signed the oath."

"Then," the official went on, "you must immediately arrest the man who fired on the patrol."

"All right," answered the *campiere,* and went away. About an hour later he came back with a companion leading between them the wanted man whom they handed over.

To judge by facts, then, things were going very well. It was now possible to go further. So I had a small brass badge made to be worn in the buttonhole: it was an ear of corn between two crossed muskets and bore the words *"La forza che difende la produzione"* And I did not make it a badge which indicated the functions of the *campieri* in general and therefore one to be worn by all—which would have deprived it of all special significance—but I gave it the value of a special distinction to be awarded to the most deserving *campieri* in individual cases. Naturally, I hoped that one day all the *campieri* would have earned it, but I wished to bring this about by gradual and selective methods and according to each man's merit. I began distributing them personally in small quantities on the occasion of public ceremonies or of country gatherings, fixing them in the buttonholes of the *campieri* whom from time to time the local police authorities designated the best, in full view of the crowd. A very short dialogue that I once had with a *campiere* was enough to show me in what spirit the *campieri* welcomed the institution of the badge. It was at the first distribution of badges that I made. The selected *campieri* were called up in a loud voice so that their names might be well heard by the mass of farmers and peasants who had gathered for the ceremony, and one by one came up on to a special platform where in full view of the public I gave them their badges with a few short and cordial words. Among others there came a grey-haired *campiere* of proud and vigorous aspect: he was in full dress, musket, pouch, riding boots and *coppola* (cap).

"Do you know what this badge means?" I asked him.

"I do."

"Do you know that wearing it specially exposes you to the hatred of criminals?"

"Begging your Excellency's pardon, I don't mind about that."

"Do you know that, once you have worn this badge you must always wear it in the sight of everybody and whatever happens, even at the cost of your life"

"I know that, and that is why I am glad to have it."

"And supposing that anyone seeing this badge were to call you *sbirro?*" (a very sinister word upon Italian lips, meaning the police agent of an oppressive government.)

A gleam came into the *campiere's* eye and he slightly contracted his shoulder as though to take his gun off it.

"Well?"

"Begging your Excellency's pardon, in that case I should shoot him."

"Bravo!" I answered, and giving him the badge I shook him by the hand.

The crowd, who had perfectly understood the short conversation, acclaimed the *campiere* enthusiastically. It is hardly necessary to say that after this nobody thought of mocking or insulting the *campieri* who wore the badge.

I did one more thing. In order to get the *campieri* more often away from the surroundings in which they were isolated and to bring them into touch with the population of the town, I also arranged that at the annual horse show at Palermo, at which the most celebrated men and women riders competed, there should be a special event for the *campieri*. And so on the track at Palermo the most famous and redoubtable *campieri* of Sicily, dressed, mounted, and caparisoned in their traditional manner, competed before the plaudits of a public of every class in an atmosphere of growing sympathy and renewed confidence.

Akin to the class of the *campieri*, but perhaps in closer relations with the Mafia, besides being a greater nuisance, more to be feared and very troublesome owing to the fact that they lived near the capital of the island, was the class of *guardiani* of the country round Palermo—that is, private watchmen of the countryside which surrounds Palermo like a girdle of green velvet dotted with gold. In substance, the *guardiano* in the agricultural district of the Conca d'Oro was a nearer, more concentrated and more powerful form of what the *campiere* was on the *latifondi*. With regard to the *guardiani*, therefore, I acted on similar principles to those on which I had acted with regard to the *campieri;* with the only difference that, while I left to the *campieri* freedom of individual action, as was necessary in the wide country districts, I imposed a special discipline on the *guardiani*, which was dictated by the need to have them always completely under my thumb, in view of their close contact with the city. And so, after the due weeding-out of old offenders, of militant *mafiosi* and men imposed by the Mafia, while individually preserving the traditional figure of the *guardiani* of the Conca d'Oro I incorporated them in a special body with commanders, regulations, discipline, controls and obligatory badges—a spray of orange blossom between two crossed muskets.

To the glad surprise of the townspeople of Palermo, on April 21st (the feast of work), 1927, in the procession of workers that marched through the city to celebrate the occasion, there appeared for the first time, armed and in column, with their flag in front, the *guardiani* of the Conca d'Oro whom I had called up for their baptism. The ceremony took place in the Piazza Politeama in full view of all the workers and the rest of the population. After a few appropriate words I read out the words of the oath already taken by the *campieri*, and ended by asking them: "Will you swear it?" All the *guardiani* sent up a loud unanimous shout: "I swear!" amid the feverish enthusiasm of the huge crowd collected in the square. The crowd—the whole of Palermo—broke out into interminable cries of joy and liberation. Three hundred more strong and brave men had come openly and voluntarily into line on our side against crime. The bloodthirsty Mafia of the Conca d'Oro lost at a stroke its strongest means of action; and the dangers that lurked behind the white, sweet-smelling girdle of the orange-blossom round Palermo were ended for ever.

# My Measures Against
# Cattle-Stealing

Cattle-stealing had for long been a prevalent form of crime in Sicily and had constituted for centuries a special danger to the agricultural development of the island. The stealing of single animals, of which the only feature peculiar to Sicily was simply its frequency, is necessarily included under this head: but the classic form of cattle-stealing in Sicily, which perhaps originated in the ancient Saracen raids and is favoured by the geographical conditions of the country and by the very primitive systems of breeding and housing cattle, was to be found in the stealing of entire herds and flocks of all descriptions of animals. The cattle-raiders of Sicily, who had become specialists by long practice, showed a surprising cleverness in capturing, carrying off and rapidly getting rid of unbelievable quantities of animals. They had a particular technique of their own and a perfect knowledge of the art of covering up their tracks.

In the course of time cattle-stealing was so perfected as to become a regular industry, indeed, the most profitable of all the criminal industries. It became a monopoly of the Mafia, under whose direction it was systematically organised with a regular network of receivers, in which the *campieri* played a large and definite part, which covered all the best cattle-breeding districts of the island and to which continuity and security were chiefly ensured by the ease with which stolen cattle could be rapidly moved from province to province. Thus the business of cattle-stealing, as it was perfected, became one of deliberate and co-operative policy. Cattle-stealing on a large scale was never committed haphazardly; everything was pre-arranged—the place, the manner and the favourable moment for capturing the cattle, the route for driving it off, the halting and receiving places, and the places and ways for getting rid of it.

In early days the cattle-stealing had the character of true theft. That is, the cattle were stolen to sell them again secretly either for work or for slaughtering. As time went on and methods improved, that sort of thing was regarded as somewhat laborious and dangerous; and the system was arrived at by which cattle were stolen for purposes of extortion. That is to say, the stolen cattle were carefully concealed and the criminals waited until the person they had robbed, either on his own initiative or at the suggestion of special intermediaries, entered into negotiations to ransom the stolen animals on payment of a fixed sum, and when that sum had been paid, the cattle in question were left in predetermined places. It is unnecessary to go into details, but it is easy to understand how much and how serious damage this entailed to the development of cattle-breeding in the island. There were times in Sicily when an animal might have to be ransomed by its owner as many as three times. And I remember that one day at a large agricultural village called Contessa Entellina in the interior of the province of Palermo, whither I had gone for purposes of propaganda, such as I referred to in the previous pages, when I was speaking to the inhabitants gathered together in the piazza and incidentally said that I knew that not a few of them must have had animals stolen, a regular volley of shouts of "All of us!" interrupted me. This meant that more than a thousand peasants were declaring they had been robbed of their cattle. Such was the state of things.

From the earliest times—and one has characteristic proof of this in the ancient *bandi* (decrees)—cattle-stealing was vigorously combated, either directly or indirectly. Direct action was taken against the persons of the cattle-stealers, the receivers, the intermediaries, and all who made use of them: and indirect action was taken by obliging those who owned animals or had them in their possession to prove at any moment their rightful ownership by special documents called *bollette* which contained a description of the owner and the marks of the animal, including in the latter the description of a special mark branded by the authorities on the animal in question and formed of two letters according to the commune in which the branding had taken place. The affixing of marks and the issue of *bollette* were jealously kept within the exclusive competence of the authorities.

Falsification and forgery were the immediate result. The cattle thieves, that is, either falsified the documents to fit stolen animals or else they falsified the animals to fit them to the documents. They would even alter the branding letters on an unfortunate animal with a red-hot nail, or they would completely obliterate the first branding with a special blister, or they would change the animal's colour by mysterious means, or they would remove its tail or add a tail to it, and so on. The thing came to such a pitch that finally both marks and *bollette* fell to disuse, not because they were useless, but because they were detrimental to the suppression of cattle-stealing. Several praiseworthy attempts to improve these things and put them into force again had no lasting success, and cattle-stealing continued to flourish in a hundred different ways and forms, the classic form of the large-scale raid for purposes of extortion always prevailing.

I determined, therefore, to face the question squarely, and settle it once and for all. The main thing was to strike at cattle-stealing in the persons of its agents and in its technique. The men were known: the technique, as I saw it, was dictated by circumstances. I mean, the technique of cattle-raiding was necessarily bound by the topographical conditions of the country, by its state of cultivation, by the succession of the seasons, and by the physiological necessities of the animals. The cattle-thieves could certainly not drive off stolen herds and flocks along the main roads or through inhabited villages or over bare uplands where all could see them, or across vineyards or vegetable gardens or cornfields or rivers in spate or marshes. And they had not only to take into account the speed, the physical resistance and the tendencies of the animals, but they had also to feed them, and above all to water them. So that the movements of cattle thieves were limited by conditions or by routes and by moments which they could not vary—paths, woods, valleys, fords, drinking-places, extensively cultivated tracts, periods of drought, the periods following harvest, the periods of lambing or calving, etc., things which were easily identifiable according to district and period.

I had studied the matter for some time and I had discovered that the habitual lines by which stolen cattle were driven off were determined precisely by the considerations that I have mentioned. And I had a sort of map made showing the regular lines of the movements of cattle-thieves. Pinned down to its points of obligatory passage cattle-stealing was necessarily immobilised: and I took this point into consideration in my initial distribution of the groups of police upon which turned the inter-provincial service of public safety that I had instituted: and I made the following experiment. On Christmas Day, 1924—I was then the Prefect of Trapani—I received telegraphic news of a serious cattle-raid committed by force of arms on an estate in the centre of the province. According to the traditional system the whole of the police in the districts adjoining that in which the raid had been committed should have been immediately put in motion and made to converge on that very place to search for the raiders. And as a rule nothing ever came of it. But I, on the contrary, basing my plans on these points of obligatory passage, gave orders that on the following day at a more or less fixed hour, a party of police should be at a spot which, as I calculated, the raiders would necessarily have to pass. This was done, and, as I had foreseen, the encounter took place. After a short struggle the malefactors were captured and the stolen cattle which they were driving were recovered.

However, I did not always proceed against cattle-stealing in individual cases: I attacked it *en bloc*. All the cattle-thieves, the receivers, intermediaries, etc., who were inculpated on valid grounds through the declarations of injured persons were included in the wide "associations for criminal purposes" of which I have spoken, and were handed over to justice. Thus automatically, with the weeding out of the *campieri* and their coming over to our side, the whole receiving system upon which cattlestealing hinged was broken down. In such circumstances cattle-stealing was no longer possible. In fact it completely ceased at once.

But that was not all. With the aim of preventing it in the future I determined to bring into force again the use of *bollette* and communal marks; and I made regulations for this in my ordinance which is given in full elsewhere and which I followed by some special, very detailed instructions.

The main features of the new arrangements were the following. To begin with, the service of branding and marking was looked at from the point of view of the development of cattle-breeding in the island and not simply from the point of view of public safety, and was entrusted to the direction of the communal veterinary officers under the control of the provincial veterinary officers. By this means the matter was put upon a proper footing and made a special demand upon the competence and capacity of the veterinary officers of the island, who, be it said in their honour, responded with the highest enthusiasm and good faith. Secondly, in strict accordance with the principle that the fight against crime should only be conducted in collaboration between the authorities and the population, instead of jealously reserving everything regarding the branding of cattle and the issue of documents to the police officials and to the headquarters of *carabinieri*, I entrusted the business to communal commissions of agriculturists who, with the assistance of the communal officers and of the veterinary officers, but on their own responsibility, were to undertake both the branding of cattle and also the signature and the issue of documents, after ascertaining the rightful ownership of the animals in question. The only obligation resting upon the police officials and the *carabinieri* was to give assistance to these commissions if they asked for it. It was quite a new system and placed clearly and directly before the cattle-breeders of Sicily the problem of defending their heritage. When my ordinance was published there were some who expressed doubts as to its effectiveness: but they were wrong. The communal commissions, left to themselves, completely understood the significance of the provisions which placed this responsible and delicate task upon their shoulders: they recognised what a proof of confidence it represented and took a proper view of the responsibility laid upon them. They worked extremely well. In a very short time under their direct control, all the animals in Sicily were branded and furnished with a *bolletta*. Here are the numbers:—

*Animals Branded in Sicily*

| Province | Horses | Oxen | Sheep | Goats |
|---|---|---|---|---|
| Palermo | 90,666 | 34,125 | 199,925 | 66,679 |
| Caltanissetta | 52,993 | 8,239 | 47,162 | 14,481 |
| Catania | 64,921 | 20,021 | 80,954 | 23,036 |
| Girgenti | 35,736 | 9,941 | 86,991 | 31,452 |
| Messina | 35,406 | 44,174 | 160,757 | 106,893 |
| Siracusa | 55,117 | 21,952 | 27,000 | 11,094 |
| Trapani | 49,847 | 6,355 | 57,688 | 9,789 |
| Total | 384,686 | 144,807 | 660,477 | 263,424 |

In spite of the largeness of these figures, there was not a single case of forgery.

The measures taken against cattle-stealing had another notable feature. In former times the fight against cattle-stealing had been exclusively financed by the Government, which often spent considerable sums on special services, increased services, experiments, etc. The tax, in truth a very small one, which the farmers paid for the branding and the *bolletta*, was not enough to cover the expenses of this special service. I arranged that this tax, light and proportionate to the number and quality of the animals, should go to form a special fund which, when the expenses of branding and issuing the *bolletta* had been deducted, should be spent in the furtherance and revival of the cattle-breeding industry in Sicily, so that the money which the breeders paid for their *bolletta* should come back to them in the way of an agricultural revival. It was thus possible for the inter-provincial service of public safety not only to give adequate financial support to technical bodies and institutions, but to take, put into force and encourage measures of far-sighted initiative in this domain which resulted in such things as the construction of a model sheep-pen and the institution of eighteen stations for the standing of bulls. Further, encouraged by the success of these measures, I stimulated the breeders to undertake a thorough reformation and the larger development of the breeding industry as the best means for spreading over the countryside that network of healthy interests which, in the material field, is the best ground of resistance against all disposition to return to the past. My words took effect; and in a short time I had the pleasure of seeing the once-deserted countryside of Sicily once more covered with flocks and herds of every kind of animal quietly grazing in the light of day, in the peace and tranquillity which had at last been attained.

The operations for the purchase of animals concluded through the Bank of Sicily, which in 1924 amounted to 7.5 millions, in 1928 reached the total of 22 millions. The one discordant note in this peaceful situation was a dispute between the breeders who were insured against cattle-stealing and certain insurance companies over the urgent claim of the former that their burdensome contracts of insurance should be rescinded now that cattle-stealing had completely disappeared.

# The Question Of The Land

I have already explained in preceding chapters how, by means of impositions, of pressure and crimes of every kind, the Mafia had succeeded in securing to itself either the possession or the tenancy of a notable amount of the best land and *latifondi* in the island at forced rates far below their value. Landed property, especially large landed property, therefore found itself in special conditions of inferiority and difficulty, and the co-operative societies of peasants found it almost impossible to get enough room for expansion to satisfy all their members. Even agricultural wages reflected the artificial state that existed in Sicilian agriculture, and that did not certainly assist in creating between employers and employed the best conditions for that collaboration which is one of the postulates of the present regime. And the Mafia, on its part, not only grew continually fatter, but had set up in many of the *latifondi* so acquired regular centres of criminal activity. Here too, then, radical measures had to be taken. However, when I showed signs of moving, I found myself confronted with stamped paper and the cry was raised against me of the sanctity of contracts. The contracts of sale and more especially the leases granted to members of the Mafia which had been made in the full regime of the Mafia were, by this very fact, vitiated from the beginning, owing to the compulsion which was implicit in the atmosphere of the time. But this was not all. In certain cases every contract had been preceded by resistance on the part of the landowners and by consequent threats, impositions or worse on the part of the Mafia. Not a few landowners had held out until they had suffered severe losses, the theft of animals, arson and the boycotting of the land in question with loss of the harvest and the shedding of blood.

Now, in my opinion, contracts extorted in this way were not contracts at all: and to invoke the law in defence of them was simply grotesque. On the other hand, to go into each case one by one by the ordinary procedure would have caused our efforts to be entirely lost among the complicated and endless meanderings of legal procedure. I therefore determined to act directly and urgently on the lines of public safety and in the greater interest of public tranquillity and production. There were not wanting those who qualified as absurd, unheard-of and irregular my claim to take charge of the situation in such a way, although it was based upon the principles of the civil code; but as usual I let them talk. I will not conceal the fact that, while I placed no reliance at all upon the civil code, I placed no little reliance upon the new atmosphere that the island was breathing, much reliance upon the support of the landowners concerned and a great deal of reliance upon my own personal action. In the ordinance which I have quoted elsewhere the question is treated by the creation of what I called *centres of infection,* meaning by these the very estates which had been acquired to the Mafia by violence and had become centres of criminal activity.

I cannot give particular cases here and will confine myself to the general lines. In substance, after the examination of each extorted contract, the ascertainment of the impositions which had extorted it, the comparison of the rent agreed to with the real yield of the land, etc., all this being done through the police authorities and the circulating Commission of Agriculture—I acted by individual, verbal or written ordinances which were differently worded according to circumstances but always directed to the maintenance of public safety and to the interests of production in so far as the latter was seriously damaged by the neighbourhood, the presence and the activity of criminals. These ordinances were definitely intended to rescind, amend or renew the contracts in question, so as to snatch from the hand of the Mafia its dominion over landed property and its control of agricultural undertakings. In this work I was assisted by a special Commission of which, besides the police authorities, the stock-breeding experts and representatives of organisations of landowners and workers on the land were members. The work was very heavy, very rapid and often dramatic. But it was crowned with complete success. The Mafia, completely panic-stricken, yielded up its arms on this battlefield also. Against only one of my ordinances was recourse had to the Court, and the Court decided against me. But the Court of Appeal decided in my favour.

In a short time, in the province of Palermo alone, 320 estates were free from the Mafia, and 28,000 hectares of land which the Mafia held at derisory rates resumed their proper value. The difference between the former rents and the new ones was quite eighteen millions. And this was quite independently of the revision of rents which, from a different point of view, was being carried out all over the kingdom by the Government by special commissions with equal representation.

Here are two very significant documents. The first is from a letter written to me by a landowner on March 21st, 1927:—

"From the day when Your Excellency became head of public safety in Sicily prosperity returned to our family. C-an estate of 120 *salme* in the district of S.M. brought us in an annual profit of 4,000 lire for more than thirty years. After Your Excellency's arrival and your magnificent defensive against the evildoers of the other side, we have leased it for 60,000 lire a year, paid in advance and free of tax. L-, an estate of 63 *salme*, in the territory of P-, which was leased for 6,000 lire, after Your Excellency's arrival was leased for 30,000 lire a year. I quote these figures, since they eloquently tell from what grievous chains your Excellency has delivered landed property in Sicily."

The second document, dated February 2nd, 1927, was a letter from the executor of a certain state and it gave the following details:—

Two lots of a certain estate had been frequently put up to auction, but nobody attended the auction (this was the work of the Mafia who prevented attendance at the auction so as to keep the monopoly of the management of the land), and in 1920, in consequence of this non-attendance at the auctions, an annual rent of 4,040 lire for one lot and 3,420 lire for the other lot was obtained by private treaty. In the year 1927, owing to the changed conditions, a certain number of bidders came to the auction from various villages and so a proper rent was obtained; the lot formerly rented at 4,040 lire was knocked down for 19,250 lire and that formerly rented at 3,420 lire was knocked down for 11,000 lire. And the writer of this letter expressed to me the immense gratitude of a man who had been born and brought up among agriculturists and was in a position to know of many other cases where free bidding at important auctions of land had become possible again. A very significant proof of the notable revival of agricultural activity which followed the liberation of the country from the Mafia is to be found in the following figures:—

The operations for a working year of the Bank of Sicily under the heading of agricultural loans, which in 1924 amounted to about 61 millions, in 1928 amounted to 154 millions; and in the province of Palermo alone the number of motor ploughs, which was 41 in 1924, rose to 104 in 1928, the number of ordinary ploughs from 190 to 800 and the sowing-machines from 4 to 64.

# *Judicial Action*

While all the measures that I have described were being put into force according to a predetermined programme and at a rapid pace, a large amount of valuable and silent work was being done in another sphere. Under the encouragement and inflexible guidance of the King's Procurator-General Giampietro, a strong group of chosen magistrates, Signors Mirabile, De Blasi, Malaguti and others, were engaged in examining the heavy and exhaustive evidence which had been collected by the officials of the judicial police against the large number of arrested persons, and in the preparations for the important legal proceedings which arose from it; and they gradually established upon the most carefully scrutinised proofs the existence of those formidable associations for criminal purposes of two hundred, three hundred, four hundred or even more persons in which for so many years crime in Sicily had concentrated its activity. This was very serious and delicate work which demanded self-sacrifice, moderation, a clear conscience and a sensitive heart; and it was done by the magistrature with a religious sense of responsibility, disinterestedness and justice; so that, when, on the finding of the Department for Indictments, an association for criminal purposes was sent for trial to the Court of Assize, one could be certain that everything possible had been done to find out the truth. When these first cases were sent before the Court of Assize, there rose once again the old doubt, given the character and the importance of the cases, lest the Sicilian juries should become subject to inevitable pressure from the families of the persons indicted. And the idea of sending cases before Courts of Assize outside the island was discussed. I had for a long time been opposed on principle to this system which had often led to the distresses of Sicily being uselessly and injuriously exposed in various places outside Sicily to juries who neither knew nor understood their complex origins: but this time I was more than ever opposed to it, and mainly for another reason. I felt that, in face of the tangible proofs of spiritual and material reaction against the Mafia in Sicily, it would be both an error and an injury to deny Sicilian juries the right of judging the cases in question. Indeed, it was necessary that they should judge them, if only as a test of the real state of mind of the island. So the trials took place in Sicily: and the first of them and the most important, owing to the number and the position of the accused persons and the nature of the charges against them, was that of the bandits of the Madonie. The trial proceeded with the utmost regularity. The injured parties and witnesses openly and courageously, in face of the accused, made their exact, circumstantial and well-founded charges; and the accused persons were quite unable to find any defence. The jury brought against them a calm, just and exemplary verdict. These trials went on without flinching at Termini Imerese, Palermo, Caltanissetta and Agrigento; and only yesterday (June, 1931), at Sciacca, on a single conviction, twelve sentences to penal servitude were inflicted.

Naturally, in view of the quantity of the accused persons and of the charges against them, the juries were from time to time called to give their verdicts on several hundred cases, so that some people threw doubts on the jury's capacity to get a real grasp of the cases and judge them with complete knowledge. But it was forgotten that all these trials lasted for several months, and that the jury for the whole of that time, through daily contact with the accused and through the daily relation and discussion of facts of the circumstances and particulars of the case, came to their verdict in a state of clear knowledge and perfect good conscience.

There were naturally cases, both during the periods of preliminary examination and after trial, of release and discharge for want of evidence or inability to prove: but here the Fascist Government stepped in by instituting a special form of *confino* (banishment, usually to some lonely island) which could be inflicted on criminals in general, and on members of the Mafia in particular. I only applied this measure in special cases, for I think that where common offences are concerned the best thing, especially for the purpose of impressing the public mind, is to bring the guilty person, whether convicted or only charged, before the judgment of the competent magistrates.

In some cases there were releases of prisoners almost *en bloc;* but though that might in part have been due to insufficient investigation, it was chiefly due to particular local attitudes due to a number of reasons—always identifiable and often transitory— which caused injured persons, witnesses, and prisoners who had pleaded guilty sometimes to retract their statements or to refuse to speak. On the whole, however, judicial action and the sentences of the magistrates and of the popular juries clearly justified the work of the police.

# The Real Victims Of The Struggle

The real victims were the families of the arrested persons, especially of the poor ones. In this matter I acted differently in different cases. Thus, for example, in the Madonie and elsewhere the families of the bandits had not restricted themselves to favouring, aiding and assisting their relations in the sense of concealing them from the searches of the authorities, but had speculated on, and drawn profit from, their criminal activities in such a way as to get for themselves positions of special privilege. Rigorous proceedings were taken against families of this kind for direct participation in associations for criminal purposes and often for complicity in specific crimes committed by the criminals related to them.

In other circumstances I acted in other ways. One evening, for instance, quite close to Palermo a rifle-shot, treacherously fired from behind a low wall that bordered the road, killed a young girl of the people while she was going with her parents to see some friends of theirs. Careful and immediate investigation proved that the wrong person had been killed; the shot was intended for the girl's father. The motive was the suspicion that he, a bricklayer by trade, had revealed, or was going to reveal, to the police authorities the existence and whereabouts of certain hiding-places which he himself had constructed some time before beneath certain houses in the district for the use of *latitanti* and criminals. This was at the time in which I was pressing criminals most hardly, and the *latitanti* of the district in question numbered quite thirty-five and had hitherto eluded search. This murder revealed the reason of the difficulty in capturing them. We had to find the hiding-places, and we found them. There were seventeen of them, varying in size, comfortable, well-concealed and situated underneath houses of the most pacific aspect; and they contained firearms and ammunition. The entrances to them could not be perceived by touch because their edges had been cemented down. And these entrances, usually in the shape of four paving-stones, were usually underneath a sofa or covered by a rug or attached to the four feet of a night table, and so on.

Having thus ascertained the state of things, we had to proceed to the capture of the *latitanti* who, by the help of their families, were in some place of safety. But this was not a case of taking action against the families, since these derived no advantage or profit from the concealment of their relations. All they did was to help them to escape the police, and that action, so far as they were concerned, was not punishable. Meanwhile there the *latitanti* were and they constituted a serious danger to public safety. So one evening I had all the habitations of their families surrounded by the police with orders to let anyone enter who wished to do so and to follow anyone who came out. The communications between the *latitanti* and their families were thus cut off at a blow. At the same time, I gave out that if the wanted men did not surrender to the authorities I should proceed to other measures. Things remained like that for three days, and for three days the neighbourhood looked as though it were in a state of siege: it was a very mild kind of siege, but, as usual, it was painted in the blackest hues by some ignorant people. Nothing new having happened and the *latitanti* persisting in their attitude, on the fourth day all their families—men, women, children and babies— were invited to get on to motor-lorries and in these they were taken to certain charitable institutions in the city where they were properly looked after and left to await events. There were seventeen men, sixty-nine women, sixty-five boys and sixty-two girls. I acted as though there had been a landslide, a flood or something of that kind in the district. As a matter of fact, there *was* something of the kind, or even worse, namely, the thirty-five *latitanti*. These, however, seeing the turn things had taken, all gave themselves up without hesitation, without resistance and without incident. And their families, after a very short change of air in the city, were quietly restored to their own homes.

As regards the families of poor prisoners I took other measures. Having collected a special fund by private contribution, I distributed adequate assistance, in accordance with the needs of each case, to the families of the most needy prisoners and to those who had babies. And there was no ceremony or other special anniversary on which there was not a more or less generous distribution of assistance to the families of poor prisoners. The most notable support and substantial contributions for this purpose were given by the Federation of Agriculturists of the province of Palermo, which, chiefly on the initiative of its president, Baron Ettore Pottino di Capuano, was most anxious, as representing the class which had suffered most from the Mafia and other criminals, to give its most marked assistance in this matter. The number of families helped this way was a thousand in all.

I made certain further efforts to cure the evil at its root. At the first regional convention of Fascist school-teachers held in the Teatro Massimo at Palermo on the 16th June, 1926, I made a clear and personal appeal to the Sicilian school-teachers to enter the field at my side by instilling the instinct of opposition to the Mafia and crime generally into the hearts of the younger generation. My invitation was enthusiastically received, and I found in the school-teachers of Sicily an army of active and ardent collaborators. The word of liberation and redemption, as though borne on a powerful and reviving breeze, entered every school on the island, and through the children slowly found its way into their families. It made the fathers look rather pensive and the mothers rejoice.

I also announced a competition for the best book written to destroy the legends and the prejudices to which the Mafia and *omertà* were principally due and to correct the mental and moral perversions that had resulted from them by setting up against them the manly and Roman conception of the citizen and giving a correct notion of the relation which ought to exist between the individual and the social order in the interest of the country's prosperity and greatness. The book, which was to be about 150 or 200 typewritten pages, was to be specially addressed to boys and suited to the capacity of the pupils of the elementary school. A prize of 5,000 lire was to be given to the best book and four other prizes of 500 lire each were to be given to the next four. The book was to become the property of, and to be published by, the Interprovincial Office of Public Safety for Sicily. All teachers and functionaries of the elementary and middle schools both public and private in Sicily might compete. The last day for sending in entries was the 31st January, 1927. But this competition did not have the desired result, probably because of the novelty of the thing and of the shortness of the time allowed; none the less, the schoolteachers of Sicily continued their good work. At the same time, with the object of keeping children from bad example and from street influences and of providing an immediate asylum for children who were in any way abandoned, I set up by private contributions a fund for the institution of an asylum for *street children*. This effort met with particular favour and, although I had refused to have recourse to the much-abused method of public subscription, large and conspicuous contributions reached me from every part. At the moment of my departure from Palermo, however, the sum collected was not large enough for the purpose, and it was subsequently distributed to local charitable institutions.

# The Results

Under this heading words are not needed: they would be superfluous. A few figures are enough, since, for those who can understand them, figures have their voice, their significance and their poetry. Here is an example which relates to the Province of Palermo alone.

*Statistics Of The Crimes Committed In The Province Of Palermo* [1]

| Date | Homicide | Kidnap-ping | Robbery | Blackmail | Cattle-stealing [2] |
|------|----------|-------------|---------|-----------|---------------------|
| Year 1922 | 223 | 3 | 246 | 53 | 51 |
| " 1923 | 224 | 4 | 312 | 72 | 65 |
| " 1924 | 278 | 5 | 283 | 59 | 46 |
| " 1925 | 268 | 2 | 298 | 79 | 45 |
| " 1926 | 77 | — | 46 | 28 | 7 |
| " 1927 | 37 | 1 | 42 | 10 | 8 |
| " 1928 | 35 | — | 14 | 6 | 6 |
| 1st Half-Year 1929 | 5 | — | 3 | 1 | 2 |

1. These figures only come down to the end of the first half-year 1929, because I gave up my office at the end of the second half-year.
2. These figures for "Cattle-stealing" only apply to large scale cattle stealing.

# The Results

Here are some more figures which give a characteristic measure of the popular state of mind:—

*Number Of Licences To Carry Arms Issued In The Province Of Palermo In The Years 1922 To 1928*

| Year | Guns | Revolvers | Sword-sticks |
|------|------|-----------|--------------|
| 1922 | 25,459 | 18,215 | 128 |
| 1923 | 18,570 | 7,012 | 61 |
| 1924 | 13,467 | 8,039 | 62 |
| 1925 | 13,455 | 9,658 | 42 |
| 1926 | 12,596 | 6,760 | 29 |
| 1927 | 9,781 | 5,317 | 22 |
| 1928 | 6,224 | 3,839 | 6 |

There is one last set of statistics for which I have often been asked, namely, the numbers of those who suffered from rigours of the law in the course of this struggle. But those statistics I have never published, and never shall. It is a long and sorrowful list of names stained with blood and tears which I shall keep for ever locked in the silence of my heart; and I have a thought of pity for the unhappy men who, through hard but unavoidable necessity, have been stricken by the rigour of the law.

They certainly bear a very heavy load of guilt upon their shoulders, but there is no doubt that the State and society have not always done all they should for them. May I express the wish that, when they have expiated their crime, they may one day come back better and wiser men to the bosom of their families to spend their life in honest toil until the mantle of forgiveness and oblivion is thrown over the past and they are reconciled once more to their fellow-men in the irresistible march which Sicily, in the name of her history, her right and her duty, has now begun towards her victorious destiny.

Here ends my book. The crowd of memories which these pages have called before my mind silently vanishes into the mist of the past, leaving a profound sense of peace and tranquillity in my heart, without doubts, without regrets and without ill-feeling. I am alone. But fixed in my mind are the noble words which Benito Mussolini wrote to me at the end of my service: "You have deserved well of Sicily, of the nation and of the government." And the face of her whom God in His great goodness made the companion of my stormy existence smiles at me gently with infinite tenderness from the frame that stands upon my desk.

*October,* 1931.

# *Appendix I*

The following is the text of the ordinances referred to previously in this book.

## Royal Prefecture of Palermo

In view of the urgent necessity to curb and repress certain activities which are disturbing the security and tranquillity of the citizens, and in view of Article 3 of the communal and provincial law, *The Prefect of the Province makes the following Order:*

1. No person is recognised as holding the position of porter, house-porter or watchman in any private house, hotel, inn, place of trade, establishment, institution, etc., except such as, on the declaration of the owner of the house or of the person in charge of the hotel, inn, or establishment, or of the head of the institution, etc., have obtained the permission to hold such position from the local police authorities, who will refuse permission to all who do not produce evidence of their honesty and their adequate physical capacity for their functions, and will revoke it in the case of any person who is guilty of crime, gives cause for suspicion or contravenes Articles 435 and 436 of the Penal Code or Article 6 of the present ordinance.

2. The granting of a licence, etc., by the police authorities to all kinds of establishments which have porters or watchmen is subordinate to the condition that such personnel shall be recognised in accordance with the preceding Article.

3. Independently of any legal penalties incurred, porters,

house-porters and watchmen not so recognised may not wear *badges,* nor carry nor be in possession of *arms,* nor receive nor take over postal or telegraphic correspondence or baggage that is not strictly belonging to themselves, nor go on to railway platforms or marine landing places to meet or accompany strangers, nor carry out the functions nor enjoy the concessions or privileges belonging to the position that has been refused them.

4. In any case where within two months from the refusal or revocation of permission a porter, house-porter or watchman not recognised as such shall not prove that he has taken other employment he may be considered an idle person under the provisions of Article 94 of the Police Regulations and, if he belongs to another Commune, he may be returned to his own Commune.

5. On the first coming into force of the present regulations the *declaration* under Article 1 shall be made to the local police authorities within 15 days from the present date for all persons to be employed as porters, house-porters or watchmen.

6. Porters, house-porters and watchmen are required to give immediate warning, as the case may require, to the police authorities, the *carabinieri,* the fire brigade, and to call immediate assistance in case of robbery, fire, accident, etc., which may occur in the premises where they are employed.

7. Within 8 days from the present date the local police authorities shall take measures to regulate the closing of entrances to houses and the lighting of passages as laid down by Article 31 of the Police Regulations.

8. Any person who, for reasons of temporary absence, has to leave his apartment unprotected, shall give notice to the police officer in his district.

9. Under pain of having their licences suspended or revoked, proprietors of hotels, inns, furnished rooms, bathing establishments and nursing homes shall not employ any persons in their service without obtaining a certificate of "no objection" from the local police authorities who shall give such certificate on the presentation of a nominal roll of the employed persons with the power of refusing or revoking such certificate to such persons who cannot give proof of their honesty.

On the first coming into force of the present regulations the nominal roll above-mentioned must be presented within 10 days from the present date.

10. Agencies and middle-men who carry on employment agencies must make a special declaration within five days to the local police authorities and keep a proper register of the persons for whom they have found employment. Agencies and middle-men convicted of having more than twice found employment for dishonest persons will incur the revocation of their licences or certificates in addition to any other penal or administrative proceedings not excluding return to their own Communes.

11. Within 8 days from the present date all those who engage in any of the occupations mentioned in Article 72 of the Police Regulations and chauffeurs of motor vehicles plying for hire must furnish themselves with the prescribed certificate of inscription on which must be indicated by the employment agency or middle-man the particular occupation in which they are engaged. The unauthorised exercise of the occupations in question will be suppressed by all legal means.

12. The enticing-in of sick persons for purposes of profit is forbidden and will be rigorously put down. Special mention of this prohibition will be made on the certificates of inscription issued to middle-men, coachmen and other persons mentioned in Article 11 above, under pain of

the immediate revocation of the certificate in cases of unobservance. Those who are known to be in the habit of enticing sick persons will be forbidden to frequent railway platforms, marine landing places, hospitals and places of public assistance, and will be refused season tickets on the railways. Apart from the proceedings and penalties proper to specific cases in which the enticing of sick persons takes the form of violence, fraud, deceit, abuse of public credulity or any other form of offence provided for by the laws, any person who is guilty of such offence, if a sick nurse will be expelled and if of another Commune will be immediately returned to it. Repetition of offences of this nature may render a person liable to be reported to the police under Article 94 of the Police Regulations.

Public establishments which are found to be frequented by enticers of sick persons will be closed. Apart from the penal and administrative proceedings incurred, doctors involved in cases of enticement of sick persons for profit shall be reported by the police authorities to the Council of the Medical Order, and if employed in the public administration or belonging to institutions, to the heads of the administration or of the institutions to whom copies of the documents proving the person's engagement in illicit industry shall be furnished.

13. Nursing homes shall furnish daily to the police office of their district a list of persons undergoing cures or lodging at them with their descriptions and, in the case of the first, with indication of the places from which they came and of the person who had brought them.

14. Apart from all liability, penal and disciplinary proceedings, the first failure to comply with the provisions of the preceding Article shall entail the warning of the offender, and subsequent failures will entail the suspension or the revocation of his licence.

15. Apart from all liability to penal and administrative proceedings, the nursing home in which traffic in sick persons has occurred shall be liable to a warning in the first instance, and for repetition of the offence the nursing home will incur the suspension or revocation of its permission to practise under the following Article.

16. The suspension and revocation referred to in the preceding Articles 14 and 15 shall be pronounced by the Prefect, after hearing by the Provincial Sanitary Council, on the advice of a committee composed of the Vice-Prefect as president, the President of the Medical Order, the officer of health of the province, the director of the hospital at Palermo and a doctor representing the proprietors of nursing homes and nominated by them.

17. Proprietors of garages (including all persons who hire out motor vehicles, motor cycles and motor lorries) and the owners of motor vehicles plying for hire must hand in a written declaration within 10 days from the present date to the local police authorities stating the whereabouts of the place where the vehicles are kept, the number, type and registered number of the vehicles and the descriptions of all the persons employed by them with the outer halves of the driving certificates of individual chauffeurs.

All changes must be declared within 24 hours. Proprietors of garages must keep a register of all vehicles let out on hire and of all motor cars held in their keeping with all necessary particulars of the time, the persons, their destinations and place of origin.

18. In addition to observing all the regulations now in force as to carrying number-plates, etc., all vehicles plying for hire or kept for hire must bear on their radiators a special and easily seen mark which shall be determined by the communal authorities.

19. The customs officials on duty at the barriers may at any time ascertain the identity of persons entering or leaving in a motor vehicle and verify the documents relating to the vehicle and the chauffeur.

20. Apart from any other penalties, failure to observe the above Articles 17, 18 and 19, the hiring of motor vehicles to persons without a driving licence and failure to obey the signal to stop given by agents of the police shall lead to the revocation of road licences, driving licences and permits to carry arms.

21. Proprietors of livery stables (including all persons who keep vehicles for hire) and the owners of carriages plying for hire shall within 10 days of the present date furnish the local police authorities with a declaration stating the whereabouts of the livery stables, the number, type and registration number of the various vehicles, the descriptions and certificates of legitimate origin in the case of all animals and the details of the driving certificates of the individual drivers.

    All variations shall be declared within 24 hours. The proprietors of livery stables shall keep a register of vehicles hired for journeys outside the radius with the necessary indications of time, persons and destination.

22. The customs officials on duty at the barriers may at all times ascertain the identity of persons entering or leaving in carriages.

23. Apart from all other penalties, failure to observe the provisions of the preceding Articles 21 and 22 and failure to obey the signal to halt given by an agent of police shall lead to the revocation of the road licence, driving licence and permission to carry arms.

24. Certificates of inscription (for drivers of carriages plying for hire) shall be refused to all persons who cannot prove the

legitimate origin of their animals and shall be revoked where persons are guilty of an offence against Article 491 of the Penal Code.

25. Passports, for the interior, licences, patents, driving licences, certificates of inscription, etc., granted by the police authorities and the communal authorities shall have the photograph of the holder affixed to them.

26. *From the 1st January next, a tessera* of personal identity with a photograph of the holder shall be granted by the communal authorities to all who apply for them. The holding of such a *tessera* is particularly recommended to those who are not in possession of any personal documents with their photograph affixed such as passports, permits to carry arms, season tickets, etc.

27. Under pain of having their licences or certificates of inscription revoked, dealers in precious or second-hand articles, pawnbrokers, dealers in fire-arms, employment agencies and proprietors of hotels, inns, furnished rooms and nursing homes shall not, as the case may be, buy precious or second-hand articles, accept pledges, sell or buy firearms, find employment for or employ persons unless the persons dealt with or employed are provided with a *tessera* of personal identity or some other document mentioned in Article 25.

Dealers, shopkeepers, agencies, middle-men and others to whom this Article applies shall enter upon the prescribed registers the nature and registered number of the document of personal identity shown by the person with whom they have had dealings.

28. Public authorities and undertakers of public works and services shall not employ persons not provided with one of the documents mentioned in Articles 25 and 26.

# Appendix I

29. Offences against this ordinance shall be punished as the law prescribes.

30. The authorities concerned, the officials and agents of public safety and the corps of the Royal Carabinieri are charged with the execution of the present ordinance.

*Palermo, December 9th,* 1915.

# *Appendix II*

In view of the urgent necessity to secure the free and undisturbed development of agricultural activity and stockbreeding in the province by restoring conditions of public safety in the country districts, and in view of Article 3 of the provincial and communal law, *The Following Orders are Made:*

1. No person will be recognised a guard, caretaker, waggoner, *campiere* or supervisor, or as belonging to the general body of persons employed in such duties, except such persons as on the declaration of the proprietor or manager of the farm or agricultural enterprise have obtained permission to carry out such duties from the authorities of public safety of the district who, after consulting the Royal Carabinieri and, where he exists, the official commanding the interprovincial police body for the district, shall refuse such permission to all persons who have been *imposed* or *interposed*, or who have not the requisite qualifications for a permit to carry arms, or who are in any way subject to or allied with criminals, or who do not give proofs of honesty, physical capacity adequate to their functions, and personal courage, or who do not fulfil the conditions of the next Article.

This permission will be immediately revoked where the person concerned is found in any circumstances that would prevent the granting of a permission, or has been dismissed for bad behaviour, or has given rise to suspicion, or has committed offences in connection with his employment, or has contravened the provisions of the present ordinance, or in cases of attack on the property entrusted to his care cannot give proof of having done all that was physically and legally in his power to defend this property, especially in cases mentioned in Article 376 of the Penal Code. (i.e. robbery, housebreaking, arson, blackmail and kidnapping.)

2. As a rule guards, caretakers, *campieri* and supervisors should belong to the neighbourhood; exceptions are only allowed in cases of proved and admitted necessity.

   They must be provided with the *tessera* of personal identity referred to in the Ordinance of December 9th; they must have effective residence in the property (garden, kitchen garden, vineyard, etc.), farm, holding, etc., or in the neighbourhood of the undertaking in which they are employed.

3. The persons in question are obliged to report immediately to the nearest station or post or party of *carabinieri* or police office and to all kinds of circulating police that are passing through the district all crimes committed in the property entrusted to their care.

   In cases of straying animals, these persons will take measures to secure the animals and to inform the headquarters or offices above-mentioned.

   At least twice a month, according to the locality, on days to be fixed by the police authorities of the district, regard being had to the course of work in progress and to the needs of the agricultural undertakings, the guards, *campieri* and supervisors shall report to the police officer or officer commanding the *carabinieri* in their district.

4. Guards, *campieri* and supervisors will answer to the authorities for the right of persons and animals to be present in the dwellings and lands entrusted to them.

   Apart from all proceedings to which he may become liable for favouring criminals, harbouring or other offence, the guard, *campiere* or supervisor who is more than twice found unable to give clear explanations on the points above-mentioned will be immediately dismissed.

5. Guards, caretakers, *campieri* and supervisors, even where employed in different properties, are obliged to assist one another in all that pertains to the active defence of such property.

   Failure in such duty, especially where it is a case of stopping malefactors or forcing them to give up animals or other stolen property, not only entails the immediate revocation of the permission, but may render the offender liable to proceedings for complicity or favouring.

6. The refusal or revocation of permission to exercise the function of guard, caretaker, waggoner, *campiere*, supervisor or of assistant to the fixed personnel so employed shall imply the loss of the permit to carry arms, the prohibition from having arms in possession, dismissal from employment, the restitution of the animals in their care, prohibition from remaining in the neighbourhood as a tenant or in any other capacity and compulsory return to his own Commune.

7. Apart from the penal sanctions proper to offences to which it gives rise, boycotting in any manner and any other action aiming at imposing or preventing the employment of specific individuals in the offices concerned or among the fixed personnel employed generally on work or custody will be punished in the case of all persons who directly or indirectly have part or interest in such offences with the revocation of the permission or licence, with removal to their own Commune, with admonition, with the dissolution of the association implicated and with arrest under the provisions of Article 154 of the Penal Code.

   The guard, caretaker, *campiere* or supervisor who refuses to occupy the position of a person who was refused a permission, or whose permission has been revoked or claimed by another, will have his permission revoked.

The same applies to the assistants to fixed personnel employed in the above duties.

8. On the first coming into force of the above provisions the declaration prescribed in Article 1 must be made before the 31st day of the current month and the permission or refusal of the district police authorities must be given before February 15th next.

9. Apart from the co-operative societies inscribed in the register of the Prefecture, persons who have been or shall be formed into a society for the leasing of land shall present before the 31st day of the current month or within 15 days from the forming of the society to the police authorities of the district a copy of the Act constituting the society with a list of the members and any other information that may be required.

10. The provisions of Article 7 of the present ordinance will be applied with the greatest severity also to cases of boycotting or any other action aiming at imposing or preventing the leasing of specific land to specific individuals.

11. The protection of personal safety and property is to be attained by a manly assertion of right, by the power of the law, by confidence in the State organs of social defence, and by direct reaction against all who attempt to attack it, and never by compromise.

Persons should therefore absolutely refuse to pay *taglie* or any other forms of tribute, should resist all impositions and renounce the habit of looking for help or assistance to any but the public authorities.

The administrations of charitable institutions or public companies who submit to the imposition of tenants or employees, or consent to pay *taglie* or other tributes, or look to equivocal individuals to secure the protection of their property will be dissolved.

12. In all cases where an agricultural undertaking becomes a means or a pretext for, or derives profit from, criminal or illicit activities, or has become the headquarters of a cattle-raiding movement, or base and receiving place of men wanted by the police or of stolen goods or a centre for illicit meetings, or exercises any injurious action on the free development of agricultural activities in the district or on the public safety the police authorities of the district, on agreement with the *carabinieri*, after consulting the competent Commission of Agriculture shall declare it an *infected centre*, notifying all the persons concerned and requesting them to furnish with the smallest possible delay explanations and justifications. On receipt of these and also where they are lacking in cases of refusal to furnish them, the police authorities, assisted by the *carabinieri* and the circulating Commission of Agriculture, shall make the necessary inquiries and take all such penal and administrative action as the situation demands such as the revocation of permissions to employees, the revocation of permits to carry arms,the sequestration of arms, goods, produce, and animals of suspected origin and the reporting of all the guilty persons to justice whatever their offences.

13. The relations of *latitanti* residing in the district who derive financial assistance or help from the fugitive shall be requested to prove the origin of the money, the objects, animals and goods in general in their possession.

Where the explanations are not sufficient, or it is proved that the money or goods in question come from the *latitante*, action shall be taken as the law provides.

14. The proprietors or managers of estates or agricultural undertakings shall report before February 10th to the respective headquarters of the Royal Carabinieri all the grottoes, caverns and caves in their respective territories, indicating their precise whereabouts and, if possible, furnishing a plan.

15. It is forbidden to plant reed-beds at a less distance than 100 yards from the edge of the road.

    Except after special authorisation by the police authorities of the district after consultation with the circulating Commission of Agriculture and the *carabinieri,* reed-beds at present existing at less than this distance from the road shall be extirpated within a month from the present date.

16. Whosoever possesses, keeps, drives or looks after horses, oxen and cows, sheep or goats in any number must be provided with the *tessera* of identity referred to in the Ordinance of December 9th.

    Waggoners must also have their surnames and Christian names and place of residence stamped on the front part of one side of the wagon.

17. The *tessera* of identity is obligatory for all persons who have been admonished, have been under special observation, have been convicts or released from prison and for all who have once been returned to their Communes by the police.

    In the case of such persons the *tessera* must be inspected and stamped by the police office or by the headquarters of *carabinieri* concerned.

18. Any person who is surprised in a suspicious attitude outside the inhabited parts of his own Commune or even in the inhabited parts by night, and cannot give sufficient

explanations of his presence there will be taken to the police office or to the headquarters of *carabinieri*, warned to behave himself properly and be given a *tessera* of personal identity, stamped.

The second offence may render such person liable to being reported for admonition.

19. The exercise of the profession of goatherd or shepherd is subject to the obligation to hold a certificate of inscription under Article 72 of the police regulations, a *tessera* of personal identity and a permit to pasture (issued by the communal authorities and stamped by the officer in command of the *carabinieri* headquarters) on which will be entered the number, species and marks of the animals, the name and address of the owner and of the persons by him authorised to take charge of the animals, the registered number and date of the *tessera* of identity of such persons, the whereabouts and name of the owner of the land where they are authorised to pasture and the indication of the roads which the flock shall take in approaching and leaving the said pasture. The flock shall be provided with a sufficient number of bells.

In any case where a goatherd or shepherd, caught feeding his animals in unauthorised places, does not at the simple request of an authorised person remove the flock from the place in question, the owner or manager of the estate, the *campiere*, the guard, the caretaker, the supervisor, and the persons employed in such duties take possession of the animals, and in the event of their assuming a threatening attitude also of the persons, at the same time giving urgent notice to the police.

Independently of all other penalties, in the above cases the goatherd or shepherd will be liable to have his certificate of inscription revoked and, if necessary, to be returned to his own Commune.

The certificate of inscription will also be revoked in case of conviction for unauthorised pasturing or for other offences of the kind.

Repetition of the offence of unauthorised pasturing will be followed by a report for admonition.

Goatherds and shepherds may not carry arms, nor when they are in the country with their animals, may they unite in numbers above three.

20. The communal branding-mark and the individual *bolletta* for horses and cattle is restored to force, and the owner's special mark and the herd-*bolletta* for horses and cattle in herds.

21. The duty of branding and issuing *bollette* will be carried out by the Communes under the control of the police authorities and of the *carabinieri* and under the technical direction of the communal veterinary officer.

22. In every Commune there is to be set up a permanent commission for prevention of cattle-raiding, of which the following shall be members: a veterinary surgeon designated by the provincial veterinary officer; eight farmers or cattle-breeders designated, two by the headquarters of *carabinieri* or the local police official where there is one, one by the agricultural syndicates, one by the syndicates of agricultural workers, one by the circulating agricultural commission, one by the provincial cattle-breeding commission and one by the mayor of the Commune. The police official, the officer in command of the *carabinieri* and the district magistrate have the right to take part in the work of the commission.

The commission, composed of persons of unexceptional probity, shall be approved by the Prefect who will appoint its president.

The provincial cattle-breeding commission may, if they wish, delegate one or more of their members to inspect the execution of the services of which the provincial veterinary officer will have the technical direction.

23. All horses and cattle born in any Commune must be marked within a year of their birth. Important animals must be marked immediately.

The marking will be carried out at periods, on days and at the place fixed by the president of the commission mentioned in the preceding article and in the presence of at least three members of the said commission who, having verified the documents proving the legitimate origin and the description of the animals as well as the *tessera* of identity of their owner, shall give permission for the marking to proceed and shall sign the *bolletta*.

24. The *bolletta*, containing the description and if possible the photograph of the owner and the description of the animal, shall be detached from a register with counterfoils and handed over after the marking and previous certifying of legitimate origin and the examination of the owner's *tessera* of identity.

The Royal Carabinieri and the police officials are required to assist the communal authorities in inquiries directed to ascertaining the origin of the animals.

25. The transference of ownership of horses and cattle will be effected by an entry on the *bolletta* made before the communal authorities.

26. Besides individual *bollette*, a general *bolletta* will be issued for horses and cattle kept in herds.

27. Sheep will be marked by their owner and brought before the

commissioners for the issue of a *bolletta* from a register with counterfoils, after the usual inspection of documents.

28. The *bolletta* must be signed by at least three members of the commission. Changes of ownership through purchase, sale, slaughtering, etc., shall be noted on the *bolletta* and stamped by the local authorities.

    The exportation and slaughtering of animals shall not take place without the authorisation of the local police office or headquarters of *carabinieri*.

29. The commission set up under Article 23 of the present ordinance shall also act as a commission of vigilance on the occasion of cattle fairs.

30. The reporting to the police of thefts, damage to or disappearance of cattle is obligatory and must be carried out as soon as possible, and in no one case must more than 24 hours elapse. The same applies to the finding of strayed animals.

31. Dealers in raw hides and their agents shall make a declaration of their profession to the local authorities before the 30th day of the current month.

    The said dealers shall keep a register of sales and purchases, and shall give notice within forty-eight hours to the above-mentioned authorities of all purchases of hides.

32. A circular will be issued to all authorities and headquarters concerned containing the necessary instructions for carrying out the duties of branding and registering cattle.

    All cattle in the province shall comply with the above regulations before the end of February next.

Notice is given that acts of recognition, certificates and attestations in general designed to prove the legitimate ownership of animals in any person's possession will have no value if made at a date after that of the present ordinance.

Apart from all other penal action, the most severe disciplinary measures will be taken against all employees who lend themselves to the issue of attestations or certificates antedated for this purpose.

33. Offences against the present ordinance will be punished as the law prescribes.

34. The authorities concerned, the officials and agents of the police, and the Corps of Royal Carabinieri are charged with the execution of the present ordinance.

*Palermo. January 5th* 1925.

www.ingramcontent.com/pod-product-compliance
Lightning Source LLC
Chambersburg PA
CBHW061728270326
41928CB00011B/2160